life & leadership.
in gratitude,
Laura

THE
EVERYDAY
LEADER

Inner Mastery, Outer Impact

LAURA DOWLING

The Everyday Leader
Copyright © 2024 by Laura Dowling

Book Cover Photo © Steve Andrews
Illustrations © Lipika Grover
Poem: A Journey to Life © Michelle Lee
Hierarchy of Needs at Work © Maslow Research Centre

All rights reserved. No part of this publication may be reproduced, distributed, or transmitted in any form or by any means, including photocopying, recording, or other electronic or mechanical methods, without the prior written permission of the author, except in the case of brief quotations embodied in critical reviews and certain other non-commercial uses permitted by copyright law.

Tellwell Talent
www.tellwell.ca

ISBN
978-1-77962-365-2 (Hardcover)
978-1-77962-364-5 (Paperback)
978-1-77962-366-9 (eBook)

WORDS OF PRAISE

"The Everyday Leader is a transformative exploration of leadership from the inside out, emphasizing the power of personal agency and self-leadership. Through practical tools, insightful stories, and a profound understanding of human development, Laura guides readers on a journey to cultivate clarity, intention, and authentic leadership. This book is an invaluable resource for anyone looking to navigate change, overcome challenges, and make intentional choices that lead to a fulfilling and impactful life. A must-read for leaders at every level who seek to empower themselves and others in today's complex world."

– Dr. Marshall Goldsmith, Thinkers50 #1 Executive Coach and New York Times bestselling author of *The Earned Life*, *Triggers*, and *What Got You Here Won't Get You There*

"In a world cluttered with overconsumption and overstimulation, this book urges us to pause and reflect on the question, "Who am I,?" so that we can move from simply "doing" to being the person we are meant to be. Laura's book is full of personal stories, wisdom, and thoughtful exercises that allow us to look inward to become our best selves. This is a must-read for anyone who wants to become a better leader and a more fulfilled human being."

– Angela Champ, bestselling author of *The Squiggly Line Career: How Changing Professions Can Advance a Career in Unexpected Ways*

"Drawing from her experiences in business, coaching, athletics, and travel, Laura offers readers much-needed insights into this compelling book on leadership. Through insightful anecdotes and practical wisdom, readers are guided on a personal and transformational journey of personal leadership and growth. This work is a valuable resource for anyone seeking to grow their leadership abilities and make a meaningful impact in their professional and personal lives."

> – Dr. Wayne Rawcliffe, Sauder School of Business, University of British Columbia

"Laura Dowling's The Everyday Leader: Inner Mastery, Outer Impact is a profound exploration of leadership, blending her rich personal and professional experiences with deep empathy and insight. Having collaborated with Laura in preparing athletes for the Olympics, I witnessed firsthand her transformative approach to strength-based leadership. Her book captures the essence of inner work, the art of engaging others, and the impact of conscious leadership on the greater good. Through deeply personal stories and a genuine, caring approach, Laura offers practical wisdom on self-discovery, team dynamics, and creating thriving environments. Her empathetic leadership shines through, making this book a valuable resource for anyone committed to making a meaningful impact."

> – Derek Covington, Olympic and High-Performance Leader, Director of InnerStride

"The Everyday Leader: Inner Mastery, Outer Impact is for anyone seeking to elevate their leadership practice. Laura Dowling weaves vivid stories and practical tools to illuminate the way for each of us to tap into our human potential, make a positive impact, and practice self-care. This book is a must read."

> – Adel Gamar, CEO & Cofounder, Gamar Leadership Group Ltd.

"A thoughtful, engaging, and practical guide for those seeking to be increasingly intentional in their practice of leadership. This book unites head and heart, reflection and action, and highlights the inseparable connection between a leader's inner world and outer impact."

> – Dr. Michelle Louis, Founder and Principal, The Leading Mind LLC

"From the very first page, this book captivated me with its powerful blend of storytelling and practical wisdom. It's an inspiring journey into the heart of leadership, offering compelling narratives supported by solid research and actionable frameworks. A must-read for anyone looking to lead with purpose and impact, it provides the insights and tools needed to ignite both the minds and hearts of others. Truly a game-changer in the realm of leadership literature."

> – Louise H Reid (She/Her/Hers), Founder, LHR Leadership Development & Coaching, bestselling author of *Humanizing Leadership*

DEDICATION

This book is for the everyday leader.

Thank you to the brave souls who engage in the practice of leadership, who are curious to explore their inner worlds and to those on a journey of contemplation for sustained performance and well-being – in work and in life.

Dedicated to Nothando, who taught me why our leadership practice matters.

TABLE OF CONTENTS

Words of Praise iii
Dedication vii
Author's Note xi

Part 1: From ME-Leading from Within
Chapter 1:   Doing to Being 3
Chapter 2:   Who Am I? 13
Chapter 3:   More on Identity 25
Chapter 4:   Talent to Strength 33
Chapter 5:   Why Am I here? 43
Chapter 6:   Values-Based Leadership 51
Chapter 7:   Where Am I Going? 63
Chapter 8:   Agency and Vision 73

Part 2: To WE-Engaging Others
Chapter 9:   The Playing Field 87
Chapter 10: Ways of Working 95
Chapter 11: People Leadership Skills 103
                The Coach-Approach 105
                Strengths/Needs Paradigm 107
                Radical Conversations 114
                Lead with Inquiry 115
Chapter 12: Learning Zone 121
                Safety Builds Trust 126
Chapter 13: Thriving Teams 133
                Team Culture in Sport 133

Part 3: To US-Thriving Ecosystems

Chapter 14: Your Impact Matters 145
Chapter 15: Leadership and Power 153
Chapter 16: Change, Transitions, and Growth 159
                Post-Traumatic Growth 167
Chapter 17: Workplace Well-being 171
                Your Career Well-Being 176
Chapter 18: Energy Management 183
                Contemplative Practices 196
Chapter 19: What's Love Got to Do with It? 199

Conclusion 205
Glossary 209
About The Author 215
Acknowledgements 217
Endnotes 219

AUTHOR'S NOTE

Whenever I sign in to a coaching call, I never quite know what will come up as the heart of the challenge in my client's world. Recently, an executive coaching client told me one of his teammates had had a stroke at the beginning of the year; naturally, my heart expanded as I could see the pain in his eyes and hear the gloom in the tone of his voice. After we took an intentional breath together, he shared that immediately following the incident, he sat down with his team and discussed a well-being tool he had adopted as a result of one of our sessions last year. This tool offered some perspective and some ways to lean into the complex topic of managing loss and transition within his team. Shortly thereafter, the same client confided in me that he had the difficult task of executing a layoff plan which would affect more than fifty employees. What a roller coaster of a year it was for this individual, his nervous system, and his leadership practice. His mind was perplexed, and his heart was sore. The ability to hold space for someone else and ourselves as we move through turbulent times is an introduction to the work of attuning to our inner worlds while we manage the complex world around us. What I appreciated most about this leader's approach was his ability to lean into the human aspect of navigating difficult changes with his team.

Changes are inevitable, no matter where you live or who you are. As people, as leaders, we are in the business of navigating transitions and managing change, and the impact it has on both our inner world and outer worlds. The *inner world* I refer to relates to our social-emotional capacities and the *outer worlds* are about how we engage in relationships and influence change in our communities and ecosystems. Agency is required here for us to progress as we navigate the intricacies of the world. Leading with agency is the ability to lean in and be curious about our inner world, how we engage others, and our impact on society.

In the last decades, I've worked with thousands of professionals, young adults, elite Olympic and Paralympic athletes, and corporate teams, and I've witnessed people move through transitions and change. As an entrepreneur in the field of human development and as a certified professional coach with the International Coaching Federation (ICF), I've helped these individuals develop agency and the skill to practice conscious leadership. Clients turn to me to help them unlock talent, build confidence, and see what they're missing in their leadership capacities. In many cases, they've lost the knack of keeping their own development and well-being, as well as that of those they lead, at the centre of their business. I help those leaders navigate the path to an extraordinary life of opportunity, growth, achievement, and fulfillment.

Life has turned me into a committed listener. I am both a student and a practitioner of human performance, and I'm fueled by the optimism needed to catalyze change and growth in individuals. In the pages that follow, I share experiences and perspectives on leading personal and professional transformation across a multitude of settings—from rural Africa to North America, India, and across Europe. A powerful amount of knowledge is available to each of us, but it is often hidden in out-of-the-way places, chance meetings, books we forget to read, and unexpected opportunities. Wisdom also comes from listening deeply to the call of the heart. And, in my case, it also comes from working with a coach who is as invested in your journey as you are. Being immersed in a leadership practice and offering that to others is my life's work.

It was only once I became aware of my agency, fully trusting my talent, embracing my life experiences, healing the parts of me that were hurting, and adopting a thriving mindset, that I knew I could evolve into something more.

You have surely experienced a change in your life because of a decision or an experience you now realize has brought you to this moment. The value of being "conscious" or intentional in our decision-making process, instead of being on autopilot, lies in the ability to navigate changes both externally and internally. This occurs so we can extract the lessons and the joy that come from a renewed perspective. While we also want abrupt change at times, such as a career promotion, a new job, a new relationship, or something different altogether, the work often lies in incremental growth. When we can focus on the small steps of growth to extract the learnings, change feels less daunting. I encourage you to be gracious with yourself in your leadership practice as you embark on the reflections that will surface as you keep reading.

I've found that being in the driver's seat of the changes that have arisen in my life has been both empowering and frightening at the same time. We feel like we are playing small until we fully step into our power. That power comes from being in the driver's seat and exercising humility along the way. This consciousness is important for leadership, as it underpins our actions and reactions and our decisions to hire, fire, or promote. It's at the heart of how we lead ourselves—through our habits and mindset—and how we impact the people around us.

This book has emerged over the years through my experience—particularly my extensive work as a professional coach and consultative facilitator focusing on individual, team, and organizational development—and the literal and figurative mountains of research I've done into best practices in the fields of leadership and high performance. It's both an art and a science to do this work of leadership; it's a complex field of work wherein we can all make great change happen. A lot of my work delves into the question of identifying the practice of leadership required to live and serve in this world. Being a leader is holistic, so I've also included stories of family life, the sporting arena, friendship, travel, adventure, and the spiritual aspect of life. Leadership matters in each of these areas. I look at the impact of leadership on our well-being and performance. And *why* it even matters.

The stories and leadership lessons I have encountered have shaped who I am and who I am becoming on both a professional and a personal level. Hopefully, the richness of these moments, as shared in this book, will invite you to question your choices and empower you to make some hard decisions *about* and *away from* the options available to you.

The words in this book are written from my heart, and I trust that if you are inspired by the lived experience I share here, you, too, will celebrate the individuals who were brave enough to work with a coach or engage in the quest of self-discovery so they could better lead themselves and those around them.

For confidentiality reasons, I have omitted client names in the stories I've used in this book. I have also obtained the permission of those who have had a significant impact on my life to bring them onto the stage of these pages.

INTRODUCTION
Leading from Within

Leadership works from the outside in and the inside out

Questions around leadership have come up for me repeatedly in the writing of this book. What is leadership? How do we define it? What does it mean to practice leadership—leading self, leading others, and leading the way in our fragile and beautiful world? Should we be calling it "responsible" leadership? Leadership with heart? Human leadership?

Leadership is a complex field. How do we as individuals perceive it? Are we waiting for others to take the lead? The role of leaders traditionally may be recognized as those who have formal authority and a position of power; yet there is also the practice of leadership that invites every single person to engage in their own leadership journey. And this is where agency comes to life. Are you waiting or are you pursuing?

Agency

A core theme in this book about leadership is agency. With agency, we take responsibility for our actions, triggers, and healing, as well as our personal and professional development journeys. The practice of agency gets us through the mud and out the other side with an overwhelming sense of achievement and fulfilment. By cultivating inner clarity, agency gives us a sense of solidity when we're going through change or periods of uncertainty. Building agency gives us the capacity to influence our own thoughts which, in turn, brings psychological stability to the face of change. By developing this muscle of agency, self-leadership emerges.

Agency is not about ego, being "better than," or having "more than." The "work" of leadership includes finding your agency and includes how you engage others, and how you relate to the community and world at large. Personally, and in my work with clients, we continuously embark on a committed relationship to become better leaders. My intention is to inspire and support my clients' development and sense of agency through best practices, tools, and stories, instilling in them the confidence to move forward with intention and clarity as leaders. If we are brave enough to look inside and cultivate agency in our leadership practice, we take back our power to contribute positively to the world.

At the end of the day, the choice to live conscientiously requires some form of change. The choice to change—our thoughts, our response to triggers, or how we make larger life decisions—implies that both internal and external transformation lies ahead. One might ask, what the benefit of conscious living is when change can be so intimidating. It is also exhilarating, depending on your point of reference. What lies on the other side of our choices to change is for you to contemplate: Growth? Evolution? Fulfilment? Alignment? Opportunity? Disappointment? Courage? The list is endless.

That is why I am writing this book: to empower you with the agency to make intentional choices that give permission for you to lead a life that fills you up from the inside out. To move away from the distractions, thoughts, and comparisons of what society, friends, or family say you *should* do and allow you to courageously seek the clarity you need to take steps, one by one, to lean into your authentic leadership.

Structure of This Book

I've organized this book into three parts:

Part 1 starts with personal leadership topics related to the self: the unravelling of our identities, and our inner worlds – values, strengths, interests, purpose, and vision.

Part 2 explores how our leadership meets our environments and how we can engage our team members at work through conscious leadership. I outline tangible solutions and the skills necessary to build healthy, productive, high-performance and human-centred cultures.

Once we have cultivated the awareness and shifted the dialogue from *"me"* to *"we,"* **Part 3** explores the impact our leadership practice has on *"us"* as a collective. This final section looks at how our leadership impacts our well-being, and why it is necessary to continuously keep well-being at the forefront of our work performance and leadership journey.

How to Get the Best Out of This Book

To ensure you get the best out of your commitment to pick up this book, I have included multiple ways to engage with it. Reflection is a skill required to maximize your leadership potential, and this book is designed to prompt you and your team to do so. You will also find tools and exercises to catalyze your journey of growth. And there are stories to inspire your heart. Take your time to reflect, digest, and go inward as you explore your leadership power and let that fuel your next step forward.

Throughout this book, I will share glimpses of my own lived experiences and those of my clients and point to transformational leadership studies. My goal as a coach is to give my clients the gift of self-knowledge so they can be catalysts of transformation for themselves and others. My wish is that you will finish this book feeling inspired and equipped with the tools to lean into the practice of leadership. Be warned that I ask a lot of questions in this book: your challenge, should you choose to accept it, is to answer them thoughtfully, and in that way uncover parts of yourself that will surprise and motivate you. It is in the art of self-examination that we find new opportunities to grow. Most— if not all—leadership books and personal development programs refer to self-awareness as the start of our leadership journey, so I will stay true to this as I also believe in this strategy.

As a lifelong student of leadership, I'm here to share what I've gathered, witnessed, discussed, and reflected on in the last decades. I hope you will read these words with the encouragement I intended in writing them.

Assessments for Your Toolkit
*Please Note: I do not receive any form of reimbursement if you sign up for or work with these assessments.

Isn't it odd we only see our outsides, yet everything happens on the inside?

Personal and team assessments serve a meaningful purpose. To grow and develop, we first need to understand who we are and where we are *on the inside*. Just like setting a goal, or travelling to a new destination, we must first enter our starting position so we know which way to go. In my practice, assessment tools have helped individuals identify their strengths and weaknesses, as well as their leadership mindset, emotional intelligence quotient, team effectiveness, and much more. As with any mechanism, the value of tools lies in applying them to the process of meeting our goals. Many of these tools are available at the personal, team, or organizational level. Throughout this book, I have interwoven reflections on how these tools can help, as I believe they add tremendous value to identifying our strengths and gaps and can accelerate our process. Specifically, I will refer to individual and team tools, such as:

Gallup CliftonStrengths™

The Gallup CliftonStrengths™ tool informs a person about their natural way of thinking, feeling, and behaving and is a way to identify individual and team talent. It's an approachable tool that helps us understand who we are at our best and how to craft our lives and work in ways where these attributes are actively present so that we are engaged, contributing, and thriving. It not only helps my clients articulate why they think or feel a certain way, but it also helps me as a coach or leader align their strengths with purpose. Knowing their team members' strengths allows a leader to ensure people are focused on the activities they are naturally inclined to perform and determine how to manage any weaknesses present in the team. This also relates to motivation. We are all naturally motivated to do what we do best—there is an element of enjoyment in completing tasks aligned with our strengths, which means we need no reminding, cajoling, urging, or reprimanding.

Using the Gallup CliftonStrengths™ requires personal and collective agency and it will move you and your teams from good to great by creating space to align talent with purpose and create paths and goals that are strengths-based instead of focused on fixing weaknesses. As a reflection of our uniqueness, it's helpful to know the chances of two people having the same top five Gallup CliftonStrengths™ are one in 33,000,000.[1]

To purchase an assessment or to learn more visit: www.gallup.com/cliftonstrengths.

Emotional Capital Report

The Emotional Capital Report (ECR) describes ten emotional intelligence dimensions required for effective individual leadership development at a specific moment in time. Emotional intelligence (EI) is like the oxygen of our being, and it goes hand-in-hand with mindfulness. This assessment relates to the way we show up for others and shows how to develop our inner, other, or outer knowing. Like any skill, emotional intelligence can be developed, and it requires intentional training. By exploring our inner world and taking a closer look at our levels of self-confidence, self-control, and self-reliance, we can learn which specific skills we require to develop agency. Let this serve as an invitation to advance your social-emotional skills to set you up for success at work, in your relationships, and in your overall well-being.

To purchase an assessment or to learn more visit: www.rochemartin.com.

Team Culture BluePrint™
The Team BluePrint™ is a development tool that provides feedback on your team's current mindset and it provides leaders with a baseline that helps them target continuous growth and enhanced future performance. As a team, you have the opportunity to create flourishing results. But teams often become dysfunctional and break down over similar issues such as lack of trust or holding one another accountable. This report provides you with the opportunity to see how individual members' experiences, and the past organizations and leaders with which they have worked, have shaped your team's mindset. My clients have particularly appreciated this tool due to its intricate depiction of team dynamics and the way it identifies the specific behaviours individuals and teams must exhibit so everyone can become more efficient and healthier, and thrive. To purchase assessments or to learn more visit: theblueprinttoolset.com.

As you read this book, consider which tools speak to you and identify which ones you want to investigate on an individual, team, or organizational level. The science, research, theory, and reach of these tools have proven them useful around the world, across all sectors: they are accessible, well-recognized, and trustworthy. However, the above list is by no means exhaustive, and there's a multitude of modalities available to you and your teams. Some tools are timelier and more applicable than others, depending on your specific goals or challenges.

PART 1
From ME

Self-Discovery—Exploring the System Within

PART 1: INTRODUCTION

If knowledge is power, then self-knowledge is the master key to your personal and professional success. Knowing thyself is a continuous practice of exploring, being, doing, and, of course, reflecting. As I have learnt in my coaching practice; this work requires moments of pause and being radically honest with oneself as you explore the soil in which your growth journey begins.

I start this journey for your everyday leadership practice from within, because when we are well within, the fruit of our lives is evident in the outer world; at work and in life. We will explore the central questions of:

Who Am I?
Why Do I Exist?
Where am I going?

Part 1 is essential for your leadership practice to learn the art and science of people development, tools that can guide your own discovery process, and how to leverage your reflections and knowledge for your own development. Working with people to catalyze growth requires a certain curiosity, and that begins with you.

Upon reading the entire book, you may find that you continue to revisit certain chapters and concepts on your evolving journey as a leader. This work is not linear, let yourself be surprised.

Are you ready? Let's go.

CHAPTER 1

Doing to Being

Your performance is more about who you are than what you do.

Wait, what? But in sports, it's about scoring goals and defending world records; in business, it's about the bottom line; and for young people, it's about the job they end up with. While it's true that in sports, business, and education, we seek finite results, what I'm talking about here is you—a person who has infinite value—as the foundation for impactful, sustainable leadership performance. Who you are is the true measure of leadership and it affects the positive influence you can have on the people around you, no matter what playing field you're on. What does your character allow for in the pursuit of performance?

I suggest that the results you're aiming for are less important in the long-term than the person who is being crafted in pursuit of the ambition. For people like me, who are goal-oriented and hardworking, this can be a confusing statement. Let me give you an example: due to my background in sports and leadership, I was invited to be part of a panel discussing character development in sports for hundreds of young aspiring National Hockey League (NHL) players. As it turns out, a study (2003) suggests the chances of going from a Canadian minor hockey team to a steady NHL career are roughly 0.025%.[2] These numbers are staggering considering how many young children (as well as ambitious parents) are pursuing this dream. While I'm all for having a goal and a dream, I am also acutely aware of the sacrifices it takes to stay on course, all while considering the emotional and psychological stages of athlete development. The human development opportunities through sport are endless. I advocate for sports pathways as a way of life with the caveat that we create intentional learning opportunities along the way. Perhaps that leads to the question, what *is* success in sport, business, family, and life? How do we define success?

Two of the other panellists were former NHL players who spoke powerfully about their journeys. They shared openly and reflected on their high-performance sporting experiences. One of them said that today, more than twenty years after his official playing career had ended, it is the memories of the relationships with his teammates that still sustain his greatest reflections from *playing the game*. The joy, the fun in the locker room, the heartache, the suffering, the resilience after injuries, the banter on the ice, the excitement, the pressure—the consistent evolution of developing himself so he could show up to perform yet another time. His advice to these ambitious young aspiring players was to stay true to themselves and do it for themselves; he encouraged them to stand up for themselves and their teammates because that is what matters the most. While he shared that his children are now at an age where they are pursuing their father's footsteps towards an NHL career, he is intentional about slowing down and checking in: is it still fun for you? Is this what you want? What's your "why" in pursuit of *the game?*

As someone in the human development and performance industry, I am all about setting ambitions high, and aspirations higher, although there are conditions to consider, such as the ecosystem surrounding those aspirations. When the goal is clear, your environment is set up for you to thrive, you feel safe and supported, you are encouraged to grow, and you're working towards something that is both meaningful and rewarding for you, then it's time to commit and focus.

Once the conditions are set and we consider the influence of our environment (more on this in Part 2), we need to exercise agency so we can learn to master the inner world of our performance. Many of the steps to do so are articulated in this book, as a way to process our behaviour and who we are in pursuit of excellence. In my experience, there are the "outer works," such as coaching and the type of environment created, as well as the "inner works" of an athlete (and business professional) that sustain people in their pursuit of excellence. These include the development of intentional habits, mindsets, and character skills that will assist you in sustaining your ambition in and through your high-performance endeavour. The cost of placing identity solely on performance is enormous.[3] For example, both in the business and in the sporting context, the loss of identity and confusion of the "self" when transition ensues can be scary. Too often, the cost of losing our "self" in pursuit of *the game* can manifest in depression and other mental illnesses.

Recreating Peak Performance

When athletes' high-performance sporting years are over, many go into hyperdrive to recreate peak performance in all or other areas of their lives to match the intensity of the satisfaction they got during their sporting careers. Some transitioning athletes stay frozen or numb to their inner worlds (and their identity) or stuck in loss-of-self territory, where they no longer recognize who they are or what their life is about. Similarly, this applies to leaders who've attached their whole identity to a particular role or title that they've carried throughout their careers. Regardless of how the athletes manage their transition, acceptance of the situation is the precursor to moving through the season of change and growth following their years in sport.

It takes time, space, and internal work to develop the emotional agility required to thrive. What role do coaches have in setting athletes up for success beyond the playing field of sport? Whose responsibility is it to inculcate self-knowledge, and personal and professional development through the sporting experience? Likewise, what is your responsibility as leaders in the workplace to set up thriving environments for teams to flourish or senior leaders to move through transitions to retirement?

Let us consider Serena Williams, one of the all-time great athletes of our era. She has had enormous success on and off the court: as a mother, wife, serial entrepreneur, and so much more. When interviewed for an article during her transition, she talked about her "retirement-from-tennis" phase. I appreciated the way she articulated her experience. She preferred not to use the language of retirement and transition, but rather language that highlighted her evolution.[4] This is an incredibly healthy perspective for someone evolving beyond the "doing" of being a world-class athlete. Surely, her next ambitions and aspirations will continue to be inspiring as she moves forward in her journey. The same attention then went to Roger Federer when he retired as one of the game's greatest players of all time. Now what? What was his process, his transition, and his conceptualization of this season of change? Was it an internal push or an external drive that led him to move on to his next chapter of life? For Roger, it was time—time to honour his body and celebrate his successes: "the past three years have presented me with challenges in the form of injuries and surgeries. I've worked hard to return to full competitive form. But I also know my body's capacities and limits, and its message to me lately has been clear. I am forty-one years old. I have played more than 1,500 matches over twenty-four years. Tennis has treated me more generously than I ever would have dreamt, and now I must recognize when it's time to end my competitive career."[5] These world-class athletes endure a process of change and transition as do the high-performance players I've supported. In all cases, there are both inner and outer worlds to consider in this season of change. As leaders, in sports, in the office, or in our personal lives, we are in the business of continuously managing transitions and change.

Alignment at Work

With the world recovering from COVID-19, with regional conflicts around the world, socioeconomic challenges, and so much more, the need to align the human system with the performance system is urgent. How can we create a playing field that sets people up for success, that allows leaders to align themselves and their talent with a purpose so they can get the best out of the people around them—be it at home, at work, or in the game?

In the world of work, misalignment between "the self" and the organizational ecosystem can lead to burn-out, disengagement, lack of productivity and much more. This in turn affects a business's bottom line and, ultimately, overall employee conditions of well-being and fulfillment. We are also seeing mental health issues on the rise in workplaces, with nearly seventy percent of all employees across North America (2022) reporting mental health challenges and only a striking sixteen percent of the global workforce feeling actively engaged in their jobs.[6] Marcus Buckingham, co-author of the original StrengthsFinder 2.0 research, adds this from ADP Research Institute, "some will tell you not to bring your personal feelings, your loves, to work. The data, however, reveals that the causal arrow pointing the other way is just as strong. *"How you feel at work, whether your work is uplifting or soul destroying, whether it fulfills you or empties you, whether it makes you feel valued or utterly useless, all of it will be experienced most keenly at home by you and the ones you love."*[7]

This ADP research demonstrates the significance of your ecosystem at work, or wherever your playing field is, and points to the importance of bringing your full selves into those spaces so you can thrive. So, do you know who your full self is? What responsibility do people leaders have for unlocking this self and identifying both personal and professional development pathways? Gallup, a world-renowned research institute, suggests that high feelings of career well-being make a person two times as likely to have high feelings of overall well-being in their life. Based on data and feedback from my clients, I can confirm that people with high feelings of overall well-being are more productive employees and better performers; this generates a greater end benefit, such as a profitable business. Taking that extra step of genuine care and investment in people does hit the bottom line and, most importantly, it sets people up for living well.

To illustrate this point further, here are some stories of executive clients of mine.

"I hate and love our conversations," my client preparing to retire told me recently. "You ask me questions nobody has ever asked and ones I've never given much thought to. You make me think." *Yes! I think, deep down inside, that's a win for me! Bringing conscious values-based leadership to life for an executive close to retirement will make a huge impact not only on their organization, but also on their life, family, and community!*

We candidly discussed his leadership legacy and next steps. When I invited this leader to name his values, he realized what was truly important to him in his last years of working before moving into retirement. It became clear that he wanted to show more care for his team members and really learn to listen to their needs—to focus on the person, rather than solely on their performance review. Together, we came up with behaviours that would allow him to live out his values and model the behaviours he wanted to demonstrate as he more intentionally chose his leadership legacy for the last years of his working life. The coaching engagement transformed with his realization that "If it's to be, it's up to me."

Moments designed to help people "know thyself" create awareness of our being. The management of this awareness is a powerful catalyst to step forward with confidence in the direction that works best for the individual, the team, the family, or the organization. The difficult aspect of managing one's awareness is first to be open to exploring oneself, and then intentionally adapting a curiosity and reflection practice to one's own behaviours. One client, in particular, shared his own squiggly-line career journey that saw him transitioning from education to serving in the military and then entering the corporate workforce in his late thirties. What was significant about this client's experience was that through our coaching conversations his awareness of how his service in the war in Vietnam had impacted his worldview; he had needed some time to reimagine himself and his values.

While in service, the mindset was about control and command, and he was told what to do and when to do it. Now, in this new corporate setting, he wanted to imagine what kind of leadership he wanted to create so he could have more rapport with his team members, coach them, and nurture their development and well-being in pursuit of performance outcomes. The shift involved moving from performance based on a do-as-I-say mentality to one focused on people. Our dialogue gave him a chance to come back to himself and re-align his values, ambitions, and aspirations with an organization that would support his desired next steps. The client was empowered to tune back into the person he knew himself to be and create meaningful values-based, people-centric actions based on living out his values, rather than doing what was expected of him without understanding what his own needs were.

When I was working at one of Canada's top business schools as a career strategist, I had conversations with young graduate students that were similar to those I have with working employees who are chasing the *perfect job*. In my experience, most of the time, they are blinded in their decision-making by a company's reputation and pay grade. What's more, most young people are paying enormous amounts of money on tuition and, in many cases, also have parents supporting their fees; they are conditioned to look for employers who can meet their expectations of paying their debts and supporting their desired standard of living.

A more impactful approach for someone with the opportunity to invest in career choices, would be to look for opportunities that would nurture their development and align with their strengths while being diligent about entering cultures and teams that aligned more closely with their value system.

The Common Threads

Because my coaching career involves a varied clientele, I've been curious to understand what executives, athletes, and students have in common. The answer comes from the multi-layered concept of the human being, and it incorporates human energy, human potential, and human performance. The commonality is the being that is at the heart of their performance in work and life. My concept of leadership provides the opportunity for high-performance people to know who they are and who they are becoming, to know why they exist and where they are going. It also makes room for leaders to know who their team members are, why they exist, and where they are going. An understanding of this provides invaluable assistance in helping people move from a life of "doing" to one of "being."

Leadership requires reflection

No matter where you are in your journey of self-discovery, it's important to know who you are and what you are looking for. It's also important for people leaders in organizations to be curious about an individual's talents and needs in addition to their desired performance outcomes. We need leaders who encourage the unlocking of human potential so people's performance potential can follow—for a healthy workforce, a healthy sporting environment, fulfilling lives, and contributions to the greater good.

Doing to Being

What have you learned about yourself in the last five years of life? How have these years changed you? What part of you allows you to *be*, regardless of the title you carry? Are you allowing yourself to be held back by what used to be true for you—an identity, a role you played, an experience that vastly impacted you? Or are you ready and willing to align yourself with a new way of being in the world?

CHAPTER 2

Who Am I?

Leadership is more than a title

During a ten-day silent meditation retreat, the facilitator began the sessions with the question, "Who Am I?," and then left us in silence, meditating, sitting, stirring, giving silence to the noise of the world, and going inward to hear what the heart wanted to share: *Who am I?* This concept of identity is rooted in the etymology of the word identity itself, which is derived from the Latin terms "essentials" (being) and "identidem" (repeatedly)—reinforcing the idea that your identity forms through habitual actions.

You might be asking why knowing yourself so well is important. Well, I have learned that knowing oneself and the multiple parts of ourselves, helps to develop confidence and assurance, a sense of peace and contentment—whether in your role at work or elsewhere in your life. On the contrary, sometimes wanting to learn more about the true self may result in painful symptoms like anxiety, not sleeping, or depression. Unravelling the stories of our identities is complex, yet the more we get to know these parts, the more we can choose which parts to continue to allow to evolve and which parts to lay to rest. Results—like performance reviews, competitions, and exams—will come and go yet the process of going inward takes courage and wisdom and *that* is your character. And your power. Getting to know your inner self speaks the truth of your soul, and when we lead from this place, your character will sustain you and will help you see that your uniqueness is your strength and your source of energy and optimal functioning. It will also help you to celebrate others and recognize the unique value of every person in your world. There is also value in knowing oneself when moving through transitions, finding belonging first within yourself, and then staying true to that self in new environments where your former "outer" identity might have shifted.

I help clients start to name their psychological construct and natural way of thinking, feeling, and behaving through the Gallup CliftonStrengths™ assessment. For example, if you are naturally a hard-working individual who likes to set goals and feel accomplished and satisfied, then perhaps you are energized by getting things done and has a need for goal clarity and accomplishment. Knowing your talents or strengths is just the beginning. What comes afterwards is the process of intentionally aiming this talent (or natural way of thinking) toward your goals and aspirations. Understanding more about who people are through tools like the CliftonStrengths™ assessment gives clues to what people do best and how energized they will be to perform. This awareness can begin to catalyze one's sense of agency; knowing who you are and what drives you helps you step into your power.

Completing a self-awareness assessment allows us to have a deeper understanding of ourselves which we can then productively apply to our goals and aspirations. This is the first glimpse into how you can cultivate agency with your uniquely designed talents and gifts. Have you taken time to name your talents, and are you using them to influence your goals and aspirations positively?

When we are at our best, we feel better, and when we feel better, we are engaged, perform better, and have a greater sense of well-being. When we are exploring identity, however, there is more to consider than just strengths and weaknesses, we want to understand the full self: our personality, spirituality, background, ethnicity, values, and so much more. This is why understanding the self —and the evolving identities we grow into as we move through changing events or seasons—is so intricate.

Who Are You?
The first time a facilitator in my leadership development program encouraged me to explore the question, "Who Am I?" I thought, *Oh, that's easy. I'm a manager, a wife, and an athlete. Yep, that's who I am.* I responded by locking on to the titles that were then in my current reality. And yet, when I really sat with the question (and I still do that), I realized that I'm so much more than the identities of the titles or roles I carry. Fortunately, or unfortunately, I learned this in many ways. When I was no longer an athlete, that part of my identity softened, and I started to know myself as someone who is active and has high-performance attributes. But when I was no longer a Mrs.—after my divorce from the husband whose surname I had taken—and I no longer identified myself that way, a great sense of confusion and heaviness clouded my sense of identity whenever someone asked me who I was.

Who am I now? As I set out on my quest to become a leadership coach, I knew I had work to do on myself before I could best serve my clients. Who am I *really*? I had to remove the titles, the degrees, and the constructs of whatever label I had adopted. Was all that my identity or were those roles I was playing? In my voyage of self-discovery, I had to move from being attached to a title to being a person, a spiritual being decorated with rich life experiences that made me who I am today.

Adam Grant, a leading organizational psychologist, suggests that *"instead of foreclosing on one identity, where that becomes the end of all of our being, we should rethink our identities and keep broadening them through our experiences."*[8] As such, we can exercise being open to a new identity as we move through transitions, so we don't get stuck in one way of being. Grant refers to this concept as identity foreclosure. This is an extremely important topic, particularly when working with clients as they move through seasons of change, whether in their careers or outside of work. If we limit ourselves to one aspect of being, then there is little room to expand on the concept of self.

So, what comprises your identity if it's not a title? It's a culmination of lived experiences, talents, strengths, character, who you are when nobody's around, and the way you are when life brings in conflict or times of stress or moments of joy and celebration. Your identity comes from life experiences and the stories we've crafted around those experiences, it comes from the voices of social, professional and ancestral influences. It first and foremost comes from your soul, before the constructs of the ego that have been conditioned over time.

One way to start to digest this evolving question is to think about a time when you've been at your absolute best or absolute worst. Since we tend to hold on to our negative experiences a little more tightly, these might come to mind more easily. At the 2022 Academy Award Ceremony, you might remember that renowned comedian Chris Rock, who was serving as emcee for the event, publicly insulted the wife of esteemed actor Will Smith in one of his jokes. Smith, a father and a role model for millions of people, responded by marching up on stage and slapping Rock in the face. Will Smith gave us a current example of expressing the worst self.

"That (slap) was not a representation of the man that I want to be," he later said in an interview.[9] We can look at ourselves as showing up as our best selves (our high self) or our worst selves (our low self); each is part of our identity and it's important to know when we are in these places so we can consciously regulate our experiences accordingly.

To gain some awareness around tapping into your best self, we have to set aside that nagging, self-doubting voice that might be saying you've never been at your best and focus on a time when you shone. For example, you might have nailed a work presentation, you made a difference in someone else's life, or perhaps you reached a goal you've been working on for a long time. The term "at your best" can take on a plethora of attributes. The reflection here when you have identified that moment, is to ask how you felt when you were in that state. What was different in comparison to when you weren't quite so high or when that pit in your stomach just wouldn't go away? Think about it honestly, write it down, and keep staying curious throughout this discovery process.

Knowing Your True Self

Knowing your true self—being able to answer that "Who Am I?" question—is a lifelong process. There is no real road map to get to an answer, either. As a coach, I have the privilege of building people up and helping them discover their purpose, vision, and values while identifying their strengths. A key part of the process is to remove the "noise"—the noise of limiting thoughts, the noise of people who aren't supportive, the noise of past failures; whatever "noise" is holding you back, the idea is to acknowledge it and override it with a future self you can move towards. That is where your wisdom lies. It can be uncomfortable and daunting to get quiet, especially for a high performer, as we spend most of our lives in System 1 – the fast, automatic doing mode. Whereas when we can create time to access stillness or a space of System 2 thinking—to think about what we're thinking about—we can tune inward instead of getting caught up in the noise outside.[10] Our culture creates little time for System 2 thinking, yet arguably that is a great need we have as human beings. To be able to go within and explore who we are we need to quieten down and that requires reducing the noise of our influences; this moves us from doing to being and reflecting.

Consider you are going to a busy market (I'm reminded of a hustling and bustling market in the centre of Beijing). You are being called in many different directions:

"Come here, good price for you."

"Come here, I have something nice for you."

"Come here—new stock just in."

Isn't this what our days are like? We're pulled by different people, opinions, ads, norms, and so much more:

"You should do this."

"You are not doing enough here."

"I need this from you."

How are you moving *from* what others think you are and what needs you have *towards* the person you know yourself to be at your best? I call this the *"From-To"* process. To do this successfully, I'm constantly looking inward and making sure my true self is being heard. In listening to all the different parts of me, I focus on continuing to develop and write—then rewrite and rewrite again—my narrative, to make sure I am fully knowing and expressing myself as my identity evolves. From athlete to student to entrepreneur to non-profit advocate to coach to mentor to yoga teacher. From being married and a stepmom to not being married yet still being a mom ... my life has had plot twists and turns at almost every junction. Regardless of the titles we give ourselves (or that are bestowed upon us!) or the roles we play, our identity at the base of who we are is deeper than the external descriptors.

We can also look at the aspects of our narrative that lie outside of titles. For example, do you believe you are the hero of your story? The person who overcomes challenges? Or perhaps you perceive yourself as the healer, the person who continuously acts in service to others in need and then finds themselves enduring burn-out and exhaustion? Or, possibly you are the victim, where you feel things happen *to* you, rather than see situations as fluid parts of life that ultimately foster your growth. Your narrative—how you see your own self, your story, and your world—shapes who you are.

These experiences of life, along with our roles and narratives, all contribute to who we are and our ability to think well of ourselves. I am a firm believer in the idea that taking time to reflect deeply and connect with a higher power allows us to rise toward purpose and well-being. This also speaks to a spiritual practice where we can tap into our intuitive selves, quieting the mind through meditation and other introspective methodologies. Then, we can begin to experience our true being, our wise self.

It's never too early or too late to start discovering who you are. Whether you are a student, an athlete, an emerging leader, or someone who has been around the block a few times, set aside any thoughts of comparing yourself to others and look at who you are and how you show up. If not now, then when? What is the story you're telling yourself about who you are and who you want to become? The science of neuroplasticity tells us that, in fact, we can rewire the thought patterns of our brains so we can change the direction of our being– to unlock unending potential for change, growth, and creativity. The choice is yours.

Our Identities Evolve

The ability to see that our identities evolve through growth and change is a skill in and of itself, and part of this process is learning to accept what *is*. Acceptance is a prerequisite for change, and this is the internal part of the external change process. I often hear clients saying, "I wish I had started this work earlier in life." And yet, while we might say that and feel it's true, perhaps our being wasn't quite ready in our earlier years to be still and look inwards. Perhaps life was happening at a speed of growth, or a busyness, that didn't allow for the burning platform for change. And that is okay. Yet, if you have an inkling that there is more, that in the days ahead you hold a vision of your future way of being, go on and take a breath and sit in the inquiry of yourself and your authentic being.

Reflective questions and work to go inward require curiosity during a time of stress and change. Looking inward is the transformative aspect of a change that actually happens externally. When one part of an identity is removed, it's scary to know where to begin or what we might do when we finish our inquiry. It is especially difficult when we define ourselves by one area of our lives.

My experience working with one particular athlete is a common one among those in high-performance sports. This athlete had committed their whole self, being, and life to their performance. After more than twenty years of committing to one identity we had to look deeper at the narratives of identity, so they could move through the transition phase of life-after-sport with more clarity and regain energy to move forward in life with new drive and new aspirations.

We started the process by putting some psychological language around this athlete's natural way of thinking, feeling, and behaving using the Gallup CliftonStrengths™ assessment. Although this is a self-assessment, it pulls out what's *not* said and gives a person language to articulate not only their natural talent but also what their needs might be. There is a comfort that unfolds within a person as they start to feel seen, almost as if the assessment knows exactly what their way of being is. For example, a person with strong communication skills may want to be in an environment where they are fully able to express themselves with an audience to whom they can relate.

After this athlete had completed their assessment, our conversations unfolded profoundly into her purpose and the specific contributions she wanted to make to society to actualize the lessons, experiences, and talents deep inside her. This conversation of developing outward agency starts deep within with a transformative aliveness that unfolds when someone can meet their heart's desires while longing to contribute to something bigger than themselves.

Typically, in sport, I look at what kind of leadership helped these athletes thrive. And ask what difference it made. In conversation and reflection, I ask who supported them at different points and if it mattered. Do they see themselves working better in a team or individually? What was their recovery and reflection process in sport and how can they apply it outside of sport? How did they show up as a leader in sport – during competition, after competition, in their community, and in their family? All these reflections are important in helping athletes identify what their needs are so they can cultivate a new environment beyond sport.

In this example, this athlete recognized she had influence. A voice. A message to share with the next generation. Stories to inspire, to give young people the belief and the agency that they too, can dream and set ambitious goals.

I Have Something to Offer

Is this athlete still an athlete? Yes. However, after our work together, she has a deeper understanding of the strengths, values, purpose, and goals she wants to move forward with when she rewires the narrative and moves from "I'm nobody now," to "I have something to offer this world." *That* is the practice of the *from-to* and stepping into the art of agency.

From "I'm so old and have never worked before," to "What can I learn and how can I transfer my sport leadership skills to a different sector?" From doing to being a high performer. The Gallup assessment showed this athlete that she had a gift for communicating and thriving in front of an audience. Coupled with a real passion for fostering change in the community, her next steps were imminent. New goals were set, and her podcast was launched to impart knowledge and stories. Remember, strengths don't tell us what you will do; they tell us how you will do it.

Marianne Williamson, a renowned author, recently gave an inspiring talk about the state of the world and the importance of using consciousness to elevate ourselves. She got a strong, "yes!" from me when she said, "Instead of asking, 'what should I do now?' Ask yourself, 'who am I?', 'who do I need to become for my next story to evolve?'" She promoted the significance of finding the answers from within, "the answers are truly found inside, in your being."[11]

So, how do you connect to this inside world? The inner voice comes to life when we can practice tuning into our stillness. As we reduce the noise of the world, social media, and the expectations of society, family, friends, and even loved ones, we can tune in and explore the whispers of our becoming. A ten-day meditation can certainly help and be life-changing, but it's not required. This work of stillness is a muscle, an exercise we need to practice daily because so much of our logical brain is consumed with the ways of the world, at the expense of giving space to the ways of the heart and being. So, what is in the way? Are you uncomfortable in your being? Your stillness? Are there limitations, thoughts, excuses, and fears lying there that you don't want to voice? That's okay. Nobody said this work was easy, yet the reward will amplify your being. The reward is purposeful abundant living that allows your true self to come to life. It's knowing in your heart of hearts, that you chose this path, and that you are powerful beyond measure. The goal here with leadership is not to seek outwardly but to grow on the inside. Your awareness and acceptance of self will inform your agency to act with purpose.

Who Am I?

Practice intentional quiet time through meditation, prayer, journaling, and reflecting on who you are called to be. You were uniquely designed for a purpose; who is at the core of this being?

- Be curious about who has shaped you, and which experiences. Who do you want to be moving forward, and what do you stand for?
- Listen to the cues in your life:
    - What energizes you?
    - What depletes you?
    - When you're at your best, who are you with, what are you doing, and what got you there?
    - When you're at your worst, who are you with, what are you doing, and what got you there?

Now let's take a deeper step into your understanding of who you are—there is always more available to us and this is an ongoing journey! We will keep exploring this transition and the evolving process of exploring *Who am I?* through this book as it informs and relates to many pivots in life, especially as we move through changes in our careers, family life, and sporting domains. It is rarely a linear process, and it requires a person to have a high degree of compassion for themselves as endings and beginnings flood them with emotional turbulence. What remains, however, is the true self.

CHAPTER 3

More on Identity

Leadership requires you to not know it all

Another way to put language around identity is by answering the question, "Where are you from?" In my nomadic life, this question penetrates my existence almost daily. It makes me wonder why this question is so common. I've come to believe that asking where someone comes from has become a way to gather insights into their culture, and it therefore helps shape a person's constructed identity. While we can have evolving identities of the self, our environments and places of origin can strongly influence our belief system and what we believe to be true about the world around us.

When someone asks me where I'm from, I pause and think for a second. How should I position my response? Is the person asking the question truly curious about my funny accent? Do they want to know my life story? Are they being polite or judging? What does it matter anyway? Depending on my mood or interpretation of the question, the story can take me less than three seconds to tell, and I might say, "Oh I'm currently living in Vancouver, Canada." Though, I rarely get away with that with my unusual accent. Other times, I will ask if they have a few minutes because it's a long story.

The truth is that I was conceived in Switzerland by Canadian-born parents with Irish roots, and I was born in the

UK. I'm the youngest of four children. After two years in the UK, we moved to Germany, and I lived there until I was eight. As a result, I speak fluent German and love all sweets made by a German confectionery company called HARIBO. Germany is where I found a love for the sport of (field) hockey that has taken me across the globe and shaped much of my life story as well as the lessons I've learned. After many years spent growing up in Germany, I moved to the United States of America (USA) before moving again to Canada at the age of thirteen. I adopted English as a second (now primary) language while living in the United States, and this is where I learned to pronounce my name, Laura, with the English intonation, rather than the stronger German pronunciation. Something that fascinated me about these worldly moves was the different perspectives shared in the history lessons I was given in each school I attended. I heard a German version, an American version, and a Canadian version of the same stories. I think this set the stage for my global mindset and for my tendency to be curiously confused, enticed, and wary of different interpretations and perspectives. Several people might be involved in the same experience, yet each can present their view from a different standpoint. I also find myself relating and connecting to different cultures in a "lived" sense; these aspects of me come alive, depending on who I'm with and what my environment is like.

By this point I pause and make sure whoever asked where I'm from is still listening – sometimes by now eye contact has wandered and I can sense a loss of interest, so I just say, "And then I lived a whole bunch of other places and so anyways, how's your day going?"

Or I might continue my story.

After our time in the USA, my family moved to Canada which was "back home" in my parents' eyes. In short, by Grade 9, I had been to seven different schools and played on all sorts of regional, provincial, and national sports teams, mostly in the sport of (field) hockey.[1] By Grade 9, I would consistently drive four hours each way every weekend to and from Toronto for practice. My aspirations for excelling at sports started in those early years, when I found myself continuously striving to be better and training with the best. Looking back, perhaps sport was the place where I felt like I belonged the most; I could easily make friends and contribute my talent for what was then my purpose. I could show up as my best self for my coach and team.

As a result of all these moves and my passion for sport, my ambitious, independent self, started to develop during these years. When I was sixteen, I learned the Dutch language over my summer holiday so I could go and play in the Dutch semi-pro league, which was the best league in the world at the time. At this point in my life I started to exercise my own agency; if I had a dream or desire, I would make it happen—even if it meant studying a foreign language and living abroad with a billet family. I also truly believe that my curiosity for learning about cultures started to flourish at this point as well. And maybe, also, my drive to belong, which was perhaps nurtured through sport or possibly through living in a European culture similar to the one in which I had spent a lot of my childhood. After a year in the Netherlands, I came back to finish high school in Ottawa—all while stressing over whether to accept offers from different universities in the USA or Canada or play the sport I loved the most. Ultimately, I decided to play in the Netherlands again: aspiring to excel and playing for the best league in the world was attractive to me. I came back to Canada and decided to move to Vancouver to start my undergraduate degree while training for the Canadian field hockey team, which was my dream at the time.

---

[1] I write "(field) hockey" because in North America that is the normal form of expression, yet in most if not all other nations it's simply referred to as "hockey."

While completing my undergraduate degree and playing for the accomplished University of British Colombia women's (field) hockey team, I simultaneously pursued bouts of European hockey again. I travelled and lived in Spain, Germany, and England, and I played some more international club games before coming back to Vancouver to earn a spot on Canada's National team and finish my sociology degree. The pursuit to play for your country is not easy, and while I suffered through injuries and a plethora of changes in the coaching staff, I had started to make alternate life plans that included academic pursuits outside of sport. When I was eventually let go from the Canadian team in 2010, I was absolutely devastated. I accepted a scholarship to play while completing my master's degree—which focused on physical activity and disease prevention—in Northern Ireland. And then, during a short stint of not knowing what to do next, I moved "home" to Ottawa, where I kept my favourite memorabilia and clothes, to determine what was next.

Life-Changing Personal Growth

In summary, before the age of thirty, I had lived in eight countries, moved more than fifteen times, travelled to countless countries, and learned four languages. I am a "Yes! Person" and whenever opportunity knocked, I answered. And so, this is how I arrived at an accelerated place of life-changing personal growth and development. Perhaps this is also why I find the topic of identity so intriguing, and I'm fascinated by how where we are from relates to our identity. What if it is our *lived experiences* in these places that shapes who we become, rather than the places themselves?

On a recent layover, I was conversing with someone about our travels. The person gently asked, "Where is home for you?" And I thought, *yes! This is a beautiful question.* I was immediately compelled to share my story, noting the world was home for me. I think as the world evolves through technology and our global consciousness, and as we become ever more intertwined in our beingness, the question of home and where we are from becomes both more complex and simpler at the same. Does your home—a person, place, or feeling of home—help you identify who you are?

In 2011, I was considering working as an instructor at a college, or pursuing a doctorate, or finding some part-time work and then—*yes!* I remember it clearly—an opportunity to provide capacity support for the Commonwealth Games Canada (CGC) grabbed my attention on a job board posting. It was a unique task, and it would be tough to decide in which developing nation I wanted to be stationed. During the interview, I remember sharing a story of how once during a tournament in Barbados I had asked my coach if I could stay on and billet with a local family so I could learn more about their world. This experience pointed out the stark differences between what high school was like for someone in a rural village in Barbados and someone attending an affluent school in Canada's capital city. The purpose of sharing this experience was to highlight the power of sport: through sport, opportunities arise to learn, to discover, to be exposed, and to be challenged mentally, physically, and emotionally. It also showed that contributing to the world of sport development was already a part of my upbringing.

Once the interview stage with CGC was successfully completed, I had to choose to either move to the African Kingdom of Eswatini (formerly known as Swaziland) or to the island of St. Lucia. And the thought process for this decision was simply, "Oh I've never been to the African continent before, so I should probably go there." I wonder, sometimes, what comfort zones actually are. Can they be confused with growth zones? And do I crave the growth zones more than the comfort zones because that is what makes up my unique DNA? I am more "comfortable" pursuing nomadic practices of adventure, exploration, living, and being than staying put and processing my life in a sedentary way.

In what felt like a heartbeat, I packed for a six-month stint in Eswatini and began working at the Swaziland Olympic and Commonwealth Games offices for the Canadian Commonwealth Games Association. I was tasked with growing sport development initiatives, facilitating workshops on healthy athlete development, and mentoring Olympic and high-performance hopefuls. When my agreed-upon placement finished, I ended up staying in the Kingdom and working for an international Non-Governmental Organization (NGO) setting up girls' empowerment clubs to help reduce the high levels of gender-based violence that were then occurring in the country. After that, I worked with local programs overseeing building and conservation projects, as well as education initiatives for orphaned and vulnerable children. Ultimately, all of these pivots in my work interests landed me in my current career, my true calling: helping others on their leadership pathway and facilitating personal development programs through navigating what it means to grow and change and live a fulfilling life for self and others. The thought that caused this shift was, *well, we can empower young people all day long, yet they will still go home or be exposed to environments that won't enable that power to evolve.* So, the shift became clear: leadership is an everyday practice for everyone and supporting people through their working lives seemed to be the clearest way for me to make an impact.

Our Invisible and Visible Identities

Identity is multifaceted. We are navigating both invisible and visible identities in our being. Invisible identities relate to our thoughts, experiences, societal constructs, expectations, and spiritual connections. Visible identities relate to our seen identities: how we look, dress, engage in conversation, and behave. Our identities are also fluid since our awareness of ourselves keeps evolving. What identity are you holding onto, and what identity are you stepping into for this season of life?

How else can we take stock of our identity? As we know, there are a plethora of personality assessments available to us today and there are good uses for each one. As I mentioned earlier, one that continued to build up and affirm my identity was the Gallup CliftonStrengths™ assessment. And I hear it on the daily when I debrief an assessment a client has completed: "Wow! That's just like me. I'm encouraged to put language around how I naturally think, feel, and behave."

Your identity is a foundational part of your leadership. Now let's look at moving from talents to strengths!

Reflect to Grow

Your Evolving Identities

Think generally about your own visible and invisible identities.

- Identify three-to-five ideal identities (i.e., I want to be perceived as…)
- Identify three-to-five unwanted identities (i.e., I do not want to be perceived as…) and for each one ask:
  - Where did the messages that fuel this identity come from?
  - Which identities feel activated in your leadership role?
  - What is required of you now in your role?

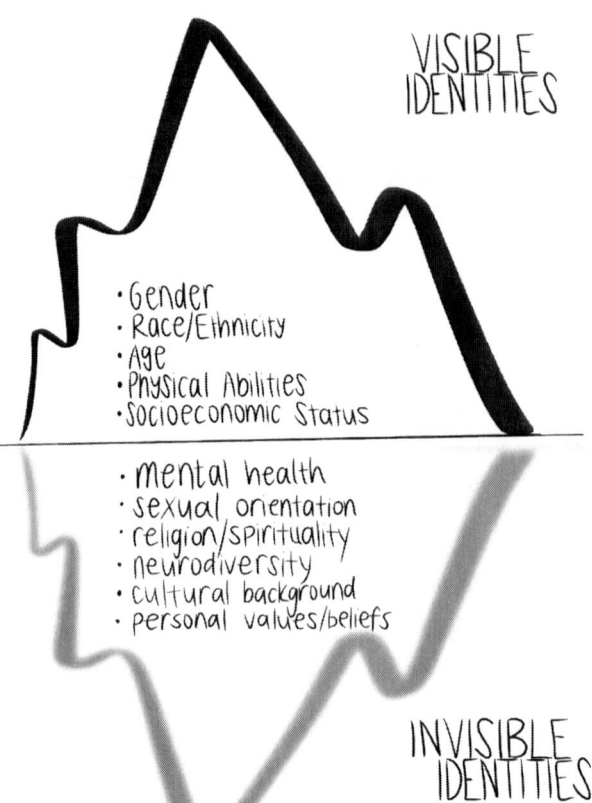

Visible and Invisible Identities

CHAPTER 4

Talent to Strength

Leadership is an act of service

I began writing this book during a time in history that has been like no other—yet when is one era ever the same as another? A time like this. A world like this. A generation like this. We have been living during what feels like a tsunami of change as we have navigated the aftermath of the COVID-19 pandemic, the demands of the new working world, the prominent re-emergence of racial conflicts creating a new awareness of diversity, equity, and inclusion, and leading our lives in new ways—all while navigating the uncertainty, grief, and confusion of our internal worlds and trying to make sense of the external. Yet, a time like this is a time for growth. A time for new leaders to rise, a time for a global wave of transformation—an awareness of what it truly means to know yourself so you can lead your best life and lead those around you.

It is a time of transformation.

Metanoia is a Greek word that means to transform from the inside out. I like it because it summarizes what I see happening daily in my coaching practice. Transformation leads to revelation. Transformation leads to uncovering the subconscious behaviours that move us from living on autopilot to living an intentional life. While autopilot living has us caught up with habits and expectations and following trends and patterns that are deeply ingrained in us (for better or for worse), *intentional* living puts us in a position of choice about how we want to show up in the world. It confirms that destiny is not written by society. This is also where agency takes root. While change is the only constant in our lives, and one over which we often have no control, *metanoia* is a choice. A choice to let the unseen boil up so it can be exposed, assessed, and then re-wired if need be. The transformation process is deep. It takes courage and is often uncomfortable, even disruptive. It requires one to live and to pause often; to go inward while the external world continues to turn. Thinking about what you're thinking about is a reflection in action. And why is it so important? It helps you discover who you truly are and what you value and aspire to. When you can look inward at your belief system and examine those beliefs that are serving you well—and those which could be limiting—you can choose who you want to be and how you want to show up in the world.

An unexamined life can consign us to living in fear, rather than in love. It is limiting to choose to live by default and get washed up with what someone once said you should do. Conforming to the ways of the world also limits your ability. By contrast, while the examined life takes a lot of work, it creates freedom and an understanding that you are in the driver's seat. And this life is full of possibilities, love, and rich experiences that are just waiting for you. The benefit of this intentional life is choice: you get to choose to live out the values that sit within you rather than those which are imposed upon you. Living an intentional life can heal our traumas, remove suffering, and move us into a place of health, well-being, and engagement while contributing positively to the world.

I propose it is time for a transformation of leadership. However, before I get into the details of transformation and get lost in possibilities thinking of how we can imagine the world as a better place, I want to create spaces in this book to pause. I have come to know the word *Selah*, the art and practice of *stopping and listening*. We know that thinking requires oxygen, so breathe. Breathe again. It's the deep exhale that gives our bodies the power to reset, rest the nervous system, and be still. *Selah*.

What follows is an unravelling of lived experiences that will spark leadership insights from every facet and every walk of life. A leadership philosophy anchored in human dignity. Anchored in love. Anchored in being better to do better. The performance will then follow.

Promoting human dignity involves recognizing that every single person has value regardless of their class, race, accomplishments, gender, religion, abilities, or any other factor. This belief is solely tied to their humanity.

The first accountability factor is this: to lead with human dignity, is to step into a lens of transformational leadership, that of calling out the good, calling out, recognizing, speaking, and drawing out the gifts within each individual person. This includes the talents and the immense untapped potential that lies inside every single human being. We are quick to call out weaknesses and imperfections. True leadership, however, begins with not only seeing strengths in others but humbly recognizing them and assuming positive intent behind the actions of people. Do you have unconditional positive regard for people? If so, how do you live that out?

Recently, one of my best friends returned to work after a few years of maternity leave. With immense enthusiasm, she left a message saying, "You know what? Someone at work recognized me for the good work I was doing and I'd never heard that before. It gave me such a boost and has energized me to refocus on my career and what I can contribute to the workplace while my kids are enjoying their school days."

My coach-approach leadership style was, and continues to be, inspired by the training of Gallup CliftonStrengths™. Don Clifton, the father of strengths psychology from Gallup, said this: "What if instead of fixing weaknesses, we focus on building our strengths?"[12] As a person who seeks out the gold in others, I thought, *yes*! *This is the way to lead life.* It has become my personal mission to give people the gift of self-knowledge so they can be their own catalysts for transformation.

My training at the Gallup Headquarters allowed me to study the talents or themes that emerged out of decades of research focussed on studying highly successful individuals. So far, the CliftonStrengths™ assessment tool has been used by more than 33,000,000 people. As previously mentioned, the chances of you and I having the same top five strengths in the same order are one in 33,000,000. Wow. This means that how we show up, how we filter our worlds, and how we lead our own lives, families, communities, and work environments are unique to us as individuals. It is in this natural way of thinking, feeling, and behaving that our value emerges.

I have coached thousands of clients, from young development-level athletes in rural Africa to Canada's Olympic and Paralympic athletes who were preparing for the Games or working through career and life transitions. I've coached graduate-level students, business owners, management professionals from all walks of life, executives in large corporations, administrators in the non-profit sector, church leaders, family members, and friends. This demonstrates the versatility, diversity, and inclusivity of a tool such as the Gallup one and also points to the excitement I've felt at having discovered something so great I want the whole world to benefit from it.

You may ask how we can possibly use a blanket approach to leadership and people management if we are all uniquely wired. Leadership must start with having unwavering positive regard for people, seeing each person through the lens of their strengths, and adopting a fundamental belief in human dignity. The most important part of all this is that our behaviours can be learned. Our beliefs and mindsets can change. It requires intentionality and a commitment to be the greatest leader you can be, for yourself and for others.

How Do You Energize Yourself?

Performing well requires an understanding of how you energize yourself. You might do this by setting holistic goals and pursuing self-actualization. Or by using assessments or tools to discover the strengths language that clarifies how you see the world, process information, and relate to others. Then you can apply your strengths to engaging in activities that serve you and others well. For example, someone who has been gifted with the ability to find patterns through data will be fascinated with statistics and numbers, breaking things down and figuring out how things work; they will lead with their rational brain. Engaging in activities at work that allow them to use this talent will cause greater engagement and more positive emotions. By contrast, someone with the strength of naturally feeling others' emotions using empathy—otherwise known as leading with heart—will be more inclined to go with their gut feeling. Both are correct, yet it's important for each person to lean into that which comes more naturally to them, all while recognizing we need each other's talents to succeed as a team.

My experience confirms that the CliftonStrengths™ assessment itself is accurate. Using it helps build my clients' confidence and sparks hope. It affirms who they are and what makes them unique, and it functions as a stepping-stone to greater self-awareness. I have personally leveraged these talents often, especially when I'm out of my comfort zone or when I find something is just not quite sitting right. For example, when I'm in a new place, I rely heavily on my instinctive curiosity. This strength quickly has me asking many questions so that I can learn and swiftly adapt to a new environment. The brilliant thing is, if you feel your energy is drained or you're not *yourself,* your natural talents can give a you a clue as to the root of why you might be feeling this way. In my case, I pay attention to why I might be depleted after spending a night out at a networking event. I'm more naturally drawn to more intimate spaces and prefer rich conversations on a one-on-one basis so it makes sense that my energy would be depleted.

What surprises my clients most is that I talk about their weaknesses as well as their strengths. Even from a strength perspective, we all have gaps in our knowledge and weaknesses, and we need to be open to receiving feedback on them. For example, at the bottom of my CliftonStrengths™ assessment, I was made aware of my weakness of extending extroverted-like energy to meet new people or speak in front of large audiences through storytelling (which is why I chose to write a book instead of going on a world tour). And, although I work as a facilitator and coach, communication is listed as a weakness in my CliftonStrengths™ report. And it makes sense to me. I'm not a person who is drawn to large audiences nor do I talk a lot. I am more reserved and prefer to work on an individual or small group basis. Writing allows for stories to be told in a less extroverted way. I do my best thinking through quiet time or writing rather than through talking things out.

I was once asked to speak at an event in front of hundreds of participants. My first thought was *no way. That is not a strength of mine; there's no way I'm going to do that.* But here's the thing: was it important to me? Yes. Was it something I wanted to do? Yes. Could I do it? Possibly, yes, with some concentrated effort. So, with conviction in purpose and a vision for success, I intentionally activated my dominant strengths and put in the effort to prepare for the event and allow for communication to flow. I worked with a coach and partnered with someone as I prepared for the event, as I love to collaborate. To exercise my curiosity, I researched and collected relevant information about the participants. Finally, I visualized my success by focusing on my own strengths and the purpose of catalyzing others' strengths. As a result, I experienced an unforgettable highlight of my career. The most important thing I learned here is that I had the talent, I knew the why, and I knew I could learn what was needed to prepare (a growth mindset). If I had let my weakness stop me, I would have missed an opportunity to give back and express my gifts to the audience.

An understanding of how our minds work adds another dimension to this conversation, so let's take a look at the Reticular Activating System (RAS). The RAS's function is essentially like a filter: it locks on to things you declare are either significant or a threat to your intended goal. If you have conditioned your mind to see the negative in a situation or to point out faults, then that is what the RAS will select and filter for you. That is what you will "see." By contrast, if you are conditioned to recognize strengths and speak out about talent, then that is what your RAS will select and filter for you. And *that* is what you will "see." Adjusting your focus will provide for a shift, not only in your energy but in those around you. For my speaking experience, I needed to filter for all my strengths, lock on to the result I desired and commit to the task at hand.

> **You cannot know the good within yourself
> if you cannot see it in others.**
> **—Zulu Proverb**

In my experience as an athlete, I found that coaches are very quick to point out what is not working rather than what *is* working. Constructive feedback plays an important part in performance improvement and there is a time and place for it. However, the research in the positive intelligence field shows that high-performance teams recognize people's strengths in a ratio of a minimum of three-to-five positives for every one negative. This is particularly important to remember due to our inherent negativity bias, which dictates that we naturally hold on to negative comments more than we affirm the good.[13] It's our responsibility as leaders, teammates, and employees to celebrate successes and strengths so our collective well-being increases. If you ask me to think about criticism or negative feedback from my sports performance days, it surfaces very quickly. It would take me longer to remember the compliments or successes related to particular moments in my career. What is true for you?

Selah

I encourage emerging and established leaders to tune inward, self-reflect, grow, own who they are, and leverage their way of being so they can step confidently into their roles and bring out the best in people so that, together, we can uplift humanity.

Having worked with hundreds of students and young people, the added value of owning who you are in a world that is rife with social media is that it allows you to be you. Otherwise, the comparison will be the thief of your own journey. Don't let the outside world take away your power as you get to know yourself and exercise agency in your own life.

The invitation for us as leaders and change-makers is to filter our worlds through a lens of strengths so we can bring out the best in our people. To help them move from talents to strengths. And to make change happen, we need to pause. *Selah*. The power of pausing lies in the fact that it allows us to *reassess our thought lives* and examine how we experience the world around the people with whom we engage. Pausing is one of the hardest things to do. Yet, in the pause, we determine whether we will build healthy or toxic thoughts, which will then impact our own mental and physical health and that of future generations. Before reacting or responding, embrace the pause and use it to your advantage. I learned this in the most profound way during that silent ten-day meditation where the exercise was literally to pause and reduce the noise of my own mind. I realized through meditation how busy our minds are, even in the stillness of moving beyond our thoughts. While we live in a world cluttered with information and noise overload, we have poverty of presence. And presence, cultivated through a pause, is one of the greatest leadership skills that can serve humanity.

We are no longer used to pausing because of modern technology and "hurry sickness." We feel guilty that we experience intense emotions that may go against reason. I felt the dramatic hurry sickness when I moved from Eswatini back to Vancouver, one of Canada's largest cities. The buses were punctual to the minute; I noticed that friends, colleagues, and others made advance appointments and scheduled their lives right down to the minute—every minute of every day. The "hurry sickness" soon became a busy sickness which led to burn-out sickness. Doing without the "being" is sickness. As people of the world, we must *be* well to *do* well, and to be well, we must know ourselves and our emotions, thoughts, beliefs, ambitions, and aspirations. The invitation for a pattern interruption is here. Creating space to pause and tap into System 2 Thinking (the slower, more conscious approach to thinking) is required in this work of everyday leadership practice. It is this practice of shifting from automatic, unconscious decision-making and reaction-based actions that will move us as a society away from our busyness and fast-paced ways of living. The benefits will be profound, and we can collectively move towards purpose-driven behaviours.

The past decade of my professional career—and the practice of being a coach—has allowed me to continuously support my clients to building greatness. Perhaps the springboard to human development is to pause, look inward, give access to the talents that lie deep inside, spend time discovering what makes you come alive, and then nurture that talent, applying and using it to contribute positively to the world around you.

Reflect to Grow

Talent to Strength

What talents or gifts have been entrusted to you? How can you intentionally aim them towards your everyday relationships, goals, and aspirations?

What are you naturally drawn to? How can you leverage your strengths in your daily life?

CHAPTER 5

Why Am I here?

Leadership requires anchors

Let's talk about meaning. Martin Seligman's PERMA well-being model proposes that meaning drives motivation and can help us move from a state of languishing to a state of flourishing.[14] I have worked with clients who are in a zone of "meh." They lack the energy or conviction to take a step forward; they have lost their drive to contribute. It's important to have grace and compassion for ourselves when we are navigating uncertain chapters in our lives. Looking inward can help us derive greater meaning from them. For example, having something to look forward to, such as a trip or an engagement with a friend, can spark the idea of something positive still yet to come. In the longer term, deriving meaning from work requires us to wisely choose where we spend our time and what we are willing to commit to; ideally, we want to commit to something greater than ourselves. Leading from purpose has a profound impact on our lives. In sport, as in life, as in work, purpose connects us to a deeper emotional drive for why we do what we do. Recently, I asked a group of national team athletes why they do what they do, and the answers were profound:

"I am here for my younger self."
"I am here to make my country proud."
"I am here for my family."

Or, when I was facilitating a workshop at a company's Leadership Summit, a leader boldly shared in front of 180+ participants the reason why he was *really* there, and that was to discover his life purpose. As we will explore further in Part 3, work that is draining or misaligned with your values will have an increasingly negative effect on your health over time. So, spending time extracting meaning from your activities and being in pursuit of purpose are highly worthwhile endeavours.

Living with purpose matters not only on an individual level but also on a team level. In large organizations, a unit or a team can sometimes feel disconnected from the end user or lose sight of why the team exists in the broader scope of the organization. The members of healthy teams know why they exist in the organization and what the team's purpose actually is. It's important to explore what would be missing without that unit or team and to ask what role it serves in the organization because leading from a place of purpose gives us long-lasting fulfillment rather than the quick feel-good feelings which come and go.

Have you ever stopped to ask yourself:

"Why do I exist?"

"Why do I do what I do?"

"What is it about being involved in sports or in this role that gives me energy?"

Is it the satisfaction of the win, the growth, the learning, the relationships, the community, the development of self or your team? Is it an internal motivator or something outside of you? The recognition, the reward? Ultimately, many motivators drive people, and it takes a moment of pause to be able to reflect and think about what compels us.

According to cognitive scientist and author Scott Barry Kaufman, the need for purpose can be defined as the need for an overarching **aspiration** that **energizes** one's effort and provides a central source of meaning and significance in one's life.[15] While Kaufman refers to one's life generally, the concept can equally be applied to one's reason for participating in sports and other concepts, such as work or family.

In Pursuit of Excellence

I once gave a workshop around aligning talent with purpose to a group of young athletes who were in pursuit of excellence. As I often do, I encouraged them to take a moment to reflect on what was motivating them to participate in sport and to remind them to look within rather than allow their peers, parents, or coaches to influence their sporting ambitions and aspirations. Finding meaning in their actions early on is a great source of power for young people, and this is just as true in the workplace as it is on the playing field. Managers need to meet their employees in this quest of discovery and help make the work meaningful.

There's a wonderful Japanese concept called *ikigai*, which means "reason for being."

Your *ikigai* lies at the intersection of four things: what you love, what you are good at, what the world needs and what you can be paid for.[16] In Martin Seligman's aforementioned PERMA model of well-being, the E stands for engagement, and this is where we tap into a flow state or an engaged workflow. It's a state where time stops, and you are activating your strengths and enjoying the challenge at hand. Being in flow is relevant to purpose as it can highlight the areas in which you might feel highly engaged. In a work capacity, this means finding what you love doing and making that your career. Every person, coach, athlete, and parent (however you define your different roles in life) has a purpose, and often we look outside ourselves to find it rather than turning inward. Both external and internal forces drive us, and the graphic image used to illustrate *ikigai* helps to conceptualize this. The beautiful thing about purpose is that it's a continuous and evolving process. One of my favourite ideas around reflecting on purpose comes from Simon Sinek's work in his book *Find Your Why*.[17] He explains that your "why" is a statement of your value at work as much as it is the reason your friends love you. It reminds us that we are who we are, wherever we are!

The idea here is that when we, as parents, coaches, and leaders, live from a place of purpose, so do our children, athletes, and employees, and it's something they can feel. When you are aligned with your purpose and connected to the organization's purpose, a level of leadership presence naturally flows. When you are out of alignment and doing work for the wrong reason, your people can feel that misalignment; they may then infer that you are not invested in either the people you are leading or the mission of the organization. More than that, being part of something bigger than ourselves makes a difference in our discretionary energy and drive to contribute. Purpose matters. And it's up to us to be curious and seek alignment to it—at home, work, or in sport.

Purpose as Fuel

I was privileged to be part of an executive retreat for the National Emergency Response Commission to HIV and AIDS in Southern Africa (NERCHA) in Eswatini in 2016. The goal of this government-funded organization was to eradicate HIV and AIDS and the Commission brought thirty of the organization's leaders together for a rich discussion of the organization's mission, purpose, and goals. During this exercise, one executive blurted out loud, "Though, if we fulfill our mission here, then, realistically, we will no longer have a job." My initial thoughts in response were, *well, yeah, then we move on to the next opportunity to positively contribute to society.* Yet, after reflection, I thought, *well, if this person's purpose was to bring home bread at the end of the day, his fear of not having a job rightfully supersedes his goal of contributing to a meaningful mission in the world. Job security is indeed a human need, and it can be a driver to getting up for work.*

Do you find meaning in your work? Is your work a job? A career? A calling? If you are in pursuit of high performance in work, life, or sport remember that where you place meaning will be a key differentiator for you.

As humans we are on a continuous quest for purpose, some of us more intentionally than others, and our purpose evolves over time. Frequent reminders of our purpose add energy to our commitments to pursue work and to our well-being in life.

When I work with clients who are seemingly lost or directionless, I sometimes need to hold space and help them find a deeper sense of meaning in their personal and professional journey. Instinctively, curiosity allows me to help people uncover the motivation, drive, and energy that will sustain them as leaders from the inside out as they find their footing again in the world—be it for their children, family, community, or other landscape. Connecting purpose with their values acts like an anchor in our ever-evolving world and greatly supports a grounded leadership practice.

Having purpose and being able to relate to it every day drives engagement, retention, and performance in all aspects of our being.

Living your purpose involves pursuing it with intentionality and includes the following:

- **Set Goals.** Goals are a primary source of energy at both the micro and macro levels yet the number of individuals who are not clear about their goals surprises me. SMART goals are specific, measurable, achievable, realistic, and timely. We must intentionally write them down so we can reflect upon them and grow. With intentions comes focused attention which in turn creates movement. If we don't set intentional goals, we repeat current patterns and may experience a loss of energy. And please remember, you can also set a goal to rest as part of your focused attention.

- **Develop Perseverance.** Perseverance requires conviction and a belief that we can achieve what we desire; it also propels us to push through to what we want, even when there are setbacks or roadblocks on our path. It is the notion of "keep on keeping on." Otherwise expressed as having grit, it is something we can develop with conscious effort and a commitment to our goals. It means showing up after a loss, it means showing up for your teammates when you're injured, and it means pushing your physical, mental, and spiritual limits.
- **Lean into Passion.** What burns a fire in your belly? Having passion is akin to holding on to the aspects of life that give you energy. What do you instinctively raise your hand to do or participate in? We might intuitively know what our passion is, or we might need to try different things to discover what lights us up. Yes, that means getting outside of our comfort zones, travelling, experiencing new activities and being open to the possibility that there might be an element of surprise in finding passion. For example, at age thirty-nine, I found a new passion for dance—salsa dance, to be exact. Do I want to make my life purpose salsa dance? Probably not, though I find it brings me much joy to move my body in new ways and bringing light and movement to my life—and to others—is part of how I can live out my purpose.
- **Live Your Strengths and Values.** These intersect at your North Star. As you reflect on your *ikigai* and bring together your natural talents, revisit your strengths and values and start to explore how they all intersect. This will be of great benefit on the journey toward discovering

your purpose. Remember that what you do can change and evolve over time, yet it's *why* you do it that gives you purpose. When we move away from living out our strengths and values, our level of joy is impacted, our well-being suffers, we are disengaged, and we can sense that this feels out of alignment with our best self. I personally value being active and living a healthy lifestyle, so I find that when I'm in an environment which does not support this, I feel disengaged and withdrawn.

Reflect to Grow

Purpose Exploration
- What motivates you?
- What positive contribution do you want to make to your family, community, and workplace?
- What do you want to be known for?
- What matters most to you?

One of my go-to reflective activities is to take inventory. Begin by taking a blank piece of paper and drawing a line horizontally across the page.

Above the line: capture three-to-five significant highlights in your life, career, or sport. When was the moment you felt proud? Accomplished? Celebrated? When did you feel you made a positive contribution to someone's life or your team, family, community, or organization? What specifically did you do? What were your actions, and how did they impact people around you?

Below the line: capture three-to-five significant low points in your life, career, or sport. Reflect on moments you endured that you wouldn't choose to repeat or live again. What were the lessons, the stories, and the experiences you can use to move forward?

Once you've gathered, reflected, and teased out your contributions, start to explore the themes common to all of them. What was the value of your contribution, and what was the impact you want to continue to make on people's lives? Then, reflect on the learnings you can tease out of the experiences you had that are below the line. What common lessons emerge here that you can learn from? Perhaps share your reflections with a trusted person, like a friend, spouse, or coach, and ask them for their perspective. Let your answers and those around you surprise you. You may learn a lot about how you've internalized an experience versus how someone else might have.

As you continue to reflect on your identity, values, talents, and strengths, your purpose will continue to evolve. You were created for a purpose, and part of the joy is discovering this over time. Let your purpose fuel you; let your vision lead you.

CHAPTER 6

Values-Based Leadership

Leadership is a practice

Values are an integral part of learning how to lead ourselves more impactfully and build agency so our everyday actions maximize our leadership potential. Values are who you are right now and who you are throughout space and time. Values are the main beliefs you hold to be of great worth in your life.

Values are the anchor in a storm. They separate grey zones from black and white zones. They provide a foundation we can count on when we need to make a decision and help steer us in the direction that most aligns with where we want to go.

Values are intrinsic to you. Your values are embodied in the way you live as an authentic leader and give you clues about what work will be meaningful for you, how you might want to best spend your time, and what activities will feel engaging for you.

From Comfort to Courage: Values

It was late August during my time living in the Kingdom of Eswatini, a landlocked country bordering Mozambique and almost entirely surrounded by South Africa. At this point in my career, my leadership development work included educating individuals, teams, and organizations across various sectors about how our minds work to help unlock potential on all levels. A client booked a last-minute, three-day team retreat for members of a high-performing team, and we were meeting in a conference room nestled in a five-star hotel. The curriculum for this client focused on developing self before leading others, and we had just started a conversation about ways to become aware of the gaps in our understanding.

I must admit I was feeling quite nervous about this specific workshop. It was only my second day back at work after taking an extended leave of absence to regroup after a whirlwind of traumatic experiences.

I vividly remember a prominent man with a large frame slouched at the back of the U-shaped table who had shown up an hour-and-a-half late (which is not an uncommon occurrence in this nonchalant culture). He was disengaged and mostly preoccupied with his phone. Regardless of his demeanour, he slowly raised his hand, unsure if it was appropriate to interrupt the personal story I was telling about what it means to experience cognitive dissonance, the impact it can have on our decision-making process, and how to resolve it. This man was a member of the top executive team and his seniority and prestige in the company and nation were slightly intimidating. I shyly acknowledged his desire to speak. My usually confident self was anxious at that moment about what he was about to say or ask. Being a facilitator, sharing knowledge, and being in front of people can be a vulnerable act in and of itself. After we locked eyes and I nodded for him to speak, the man lowered his hand, put his phone down, closed his workbook and pushed it to the side of the table. He sat up, straightened himself out while adjusting his tie, leaned in, paused for what felt like a minute, though surely it was only a second, and said:

"Excuse me, ma'am, you should write a book about this. Your experience, your courage, and the depth of vulnerability you have just demonstrated are something many women and men of this nation can learn from."

With a confused grin on my face, I realized the room was silent and nobody was moving or speaking. I took note of the eyes fixated on me and realized I had publicly shared for the first time what was then the rawest part of my story. The details revolved around the courage it had taken me to walk away from a marriage in a deeply patriarchal Christian culture.

At that moment, I felt empowered. I felt liberated. I felt I had owned my story (thank you, Brené Brown and *Rising Strong!*[18]). I felt courage on a whole new level. The story I had shared was less about the heartache and messiness of the divorce and more about the courage to share so that others, too, could feel encouraged to be true to themselves.

At that moment, I realized my lived experience wasn't about me. It was about what I could share with others so they could rise to become better human beings—and that was a new opportunity for growth for me. What if, in our pain, lies a promise? What if in our realities of joy or suffering lie our opportunities for expansion of consciousness, to raise leaders who know themselves, who are true to their values and who give space for their people to connect through the power of vulnerability?

At that moment, I discovered what it meant to be true to myself and shared a life lesson leaders could relate to. Why was that possible? Because leaders are human. Leaders feel. They have raw emotions. They have families. They have beliefs and values. They are human beings before they are business professionals, even if they are sometimes disguised in lavish lifestyles. We are all leaders, and the best of us cannot only recognize emotions in ourselves but also create space to feel what others may be feeling. This is what leadership is. Being human. Being able to connect. Being able to inspire others by first knowing ourselves. When we know who we are and what we stand for, we bring clarity and conviction to how we show up and what we want to contribute to the world. I want to celebrate and encourage the type of leadership that brings out the best in people, a way of being that celebrates our unique way of thinking, feeling, and behaving.

> ***Our performance is more about who we are than what we do. It's worth repeating.***

When I am asked to facilitate an experience for a group of people, I am in the spotlight. All eyes, ears, and hearts are on me. It requires courage and frequent personal affirmation for me to reflect my own competence—a competence that settled more emphatically around me after the executive's comment because I knew I had his attention. The rest of the morning went on successfully and we completed the workshop on the high vibration I'm accustomed to experiencing in these situations. I remember to this day that at that moment I thought I could be more of who I am; I could go out and change the world. I remember celebrating myself after the session by journaling my experience (keeping the self-talk positive) and just acknowledging how powerful it is to be vulnerable. This is how we connect with people. Sharing that moment of truth connected me to a leader who had seemed to be disengaged from an experience I was facilitating around leadership.

Stories Carry Emotion

Stories carry emotion, and through the art of aspiring to become a world-class facilitator, I have learned that stories are what people remember. So, whenever a new idea or concept is introduced, I remember to tell a story. Interestingly enough, I had not planned to tell that particular story at this facilitation retreat. However, the story I told was about what it means to choose to have the courage to be true to yourself, to know and live your values, rather than choosing comfort and the easier way out of a complex situation. We don't want to feel uncomfortable with the difficult choice. We want the comfort of continuing on the familiar path, even though, deep down inside, we know things shouldn't be *this* way.

The story I told was about the total dissonance I had been feeling during my marriage between my commitment to the person I had chosen to marry and the covenant I had made to my commitment to my faith on the one hand and the stark reality of the unhealthy and unwholesome life I was living with my husband on the other. I was also living in a country which did not easily excuse divorce, and I knew leaving my marriage would involve a public form of humiliation reflecting how I had disappointed my community. I would be perceived as a failure, someone who had betrayed their own family values. And I would need to completely reassess my identity. Was it worth the agony, heartache, financial implications, and so much more to make a difficult, uncomfortable choice? Or should I just stay in the marriage because, well, it was *easier*?

To resolve the feeling of dissonance, we need to make a decision. Once we have made a decision, we often find reassurance in the choices we think we should make so it feels like validation or it's easier because he/she/they said so. For example, you decide to buy a car and would feel much more validated if others supported your choice of the car you purchased. The discomfort of the walk of dissonance in big life decisions is that it takes a moment of pause to get quiet, to receive counsel from trusted advisors, to seek your source of wisdom from within and to be confidently able to continue to walk it out.

Living in a space of constant cognitive dissonance over big life decisions is not healthy for the mind, heart, or body. In the case of my faltering marriage, it came to occupy my every moment. I was constantly judging and perceiving, negotiating with myself and questioning all of my own and my partner's actions. The truth is, I didn't know myself back then—who I was, what I valued—and yet, during the years of marriage, I found my life purpose, which then led me to make some hard decisions.

When we are living in dissonance, we feel the tension in our system—it's like living in limbo. We don't decide or weigh our options—the pros and cons—which prevents us from moving forward. Living in dissonance keeps us stuck, and that is no way to live. To grow, learn, and develop, we must make decisions. We must take risks and learn from our experiences. Otherwise, we keep repeating the same old script. Being stuck is not an option for me, and I want to encourage you to dare beyond the comfort of staying where you are: you know there is more inside of you. There is more life to live, more beauty to experience, more growth to endure, and more love to give and to receive. We need to make choices and have the confidence to trust ourselves before others, which leads to a new way of living and being.

We can experience micro-moments of mental tension for all the tiny decisions we make in our lives, let alone the larger, more significant decisions that can change the course of our lives. On the contrary, cognitive dissonance is also a healthy experience. The act of making a decision and seeing it through causes creative tension within our system, but to do so, we require reassurance and justification for the decision we end up making. One way to do this is to focus on the reasons for the benefits of making the decision you have taken, rather than focusing on the other choices, and then take yourself through the mental rehearsal of seeing the decision through. Can you imagine what the desired outcome will be like? What will it feel like, look like, taste like, and smell like? What do you notice? Who will you become in the process? What will you have more of or less of?

Ultimately, choosing to resolve dissonance requires a decision to be made, and we can't *exactly* know what the outcome will be until we start to walk it out. That being said, we *can* have faith that everything is always working out for us. So, in the end, after a few short years of marriage and many months of dissonance, after receiving counsel from those in favour of abiding by religious rules and the influence of close friends, I chose to have the courage to live out my values, which meant choosing against a deep-rooted belief I held against being divorced and what I had always thought that meant about my relationship with God.

What Is Important to You?

You can choose courage, or you can choose comfort, but you can't have both. You are the anchor in the decision-making process. So, what is most important to you?

I could no longer stay in the so-called comfort of the dissonance that was hurting me. What was in it for me? *This is not comfort*, I used to think. The deciding factor in resolving the dissonance in the case of my marriage was to look inward and recognize what I stood for. What values represent the guiding principles of my life? It's only here in this deep reflection that I was able to identify my values, learn what behaviours would affirm these values, and align them to my goals and aspirations in life. I had been living in conflict for more than fifteen months before I had a revelation about which direction I wanted my life to take.

This was difficult. Was I being selfish by staying true to my values? What was this process of aligning values within partnerships? Why had I never previously determined what my values were?

You see, when we are in a committed relationship—for example, a romance, a friendship or family situation, a working partnership, etc.—there will undoubtedly come a point of pain or conflict. At that point, it will be our guiding principles—our values—which will determine the quality of that connection and whether or not we can continue to walk together toward the same goals. Neither outcome is right nor wrong. However, if we can look at the decisions we make in our lives as neutral and then shape our decisions based on our values and visions, we can free ourselves from what society, family, and culture expect of us. That is power.

The man who interrupted my story turned out to be one of the King's advisors, a position which is highly regarded in the nation. I have since excused his slouchy demeanour and late arrival. After the comment he made, he became actively engaged in the workshop, even to the point of sitting at the front of the room. It was a transformational experience for me.

Reflect to Grow

Personal Values Exploration

Values offer a gentle way to start to look inside. We can take an inventory of our values through moments of growth and change, or even simply when we're curious and ready to examine ourselves deeper.

- What's most important to you when you think of your life right now?
- What activities give you energy?
- When do you feel connected to others?
- Are there particular activities in which you find pure joy?
- What do you look forward to in your day, week, or year?
- When you're with friends or family, what matters and how you feel around the people you love?

We can also use values to explore our careers (More to Come on this in Chapter 17):

- Is your career connected to your personal values? Are they the same or different?
- Do you value connection or autonomy in the workplace? Or both?
- What would be a requirement for you to make a career shift?

What you feel in answering these questions is about choice. When you choose to stay true to your values, find ways to actualize them by thinking about the behaviours that best embody the value.

I remember someone saying that we can't teach values, but we can catch them. Notice the behaviours that you align with. What about them resonates with you? What don't you resonate with? Sometimes it's even easier to notice the behaviours we don't agree with as a way to further discover what we do want for our life and way of being. This also becomes part of our leadership practice in a team setting or in a new relationship.

To take the first step, create a short three-column list, like this:

What do you like about the way you or someone you admire behaves?	What don't you like about the way you or someone else behaves?	Why is this important for you?

The third column will give some insight into what matters most to you.

And, if you're stuck, here is a non-exhaustive list of values to begin:

Authenticity	Evolution	Loyalty
Abundance	Faith	Openness
Accountability	Family	Optimism
Adventure	Flexibility	Passion
Autonomy	Focus	Presence
Acceptance	Freedom	Productivity
Balance	Growth	Peace
Beauty	Generosity	Play
Compassion	Grace	Respect
Community	Health	Responsibility
Creativity	Honesty	Safety
Collaboration	Humor	Service
Community	Humility	Spirituality
Connection	Integrity	Sustainability
Consistency	Inspiration	Stability
Commitment	Impact	Structure
Devotion	Justice	Support
Determination	Joy	Trust
Expression	Kindness	Transformation
Excellence	Learning	Wealth
Equity	Love	Well-being

Narrow your list down to your top five values. For example, health, autonomy, freedom, joy, and community. Do some connect to others? Are there similarities or differences between them? What aspects of your life and behaviours demonstrate your values?

Okay, let's take it one step further. Let's suppose you were on a plane, on a journey of a lifetime, and you could take these five values with you as five pieces of luggage. Suddenly, due to a sudden detour, the plane quickly stops on the island of Mauritius (a great place for a stopover!). Now, you can only carry three pieces of luggage forward, not five. What three core values would you commit to? Which ones would you feel most aligned with? Which are negotiable and which are non-negotiable? Revisit these often, let them evolve, and check that you embody your values in all areas of your life so your best self can transcend. We are evolving beings, continuously growing and changing through our experiences which means our value system can evolve in different phases of life and through life circumstances. You may also find that you have aspirational career values that may differ from the values you carry in your personal life. Working as a coach, I find my value systems intersect at personal and professional borders with some minor discrepancies.

Beliefs. Thoughts. Feelings. Choices. Action. What will your "greater" self allow you to be and do?

So far on this journey of personal mastery, we have reflected on identity, purpose, and values, and now I want to invite some thoughts on *direction*. Where are you going? Knowing who you are and what you stand for is one thing. To move a deeper level with this self-knowledge, aim it toward your actions, dreams and desires. After all, life is for living, and vision inspires hope and direction.

The best is yet to come.

CHAPTER 7

Where Am I Going?

Leadership inspires

One morning, while I was attending the Global Leadership Summit in the Kingdom of Eswatini, I was gratified to find that one of the speakers, Sibusiso Vilane, completely inspired me. He was the first black African man to summit Mount Everest and he did it *twice*. I can still feel the emotion I experienced when I heard his story. His short and powerful book, *To the Top, from Nowhere,* roused my love of exploring mountains.[19] His experiences demonstrate an inspirational journey from a childhood living in the fields of Eswatini to becoming motivated by a friend to jet out on the quest to climb the Seven Summits of the World. He probably doesn't know this now but that morning, while I was listening to his experiences, he planted the seed that inspired me to summit Mount Kilimanjaro, also known as Uhuru Peak. This was something I accomplished two years later. Also known as the Roof of Africa, Mount Kilimanjaro is the highest free-standing mountain in the world, standing at 5,985 meters /19,635 feet tall. I had been living in Africa for nearly seven years by this time, and it was a thrill to conquer the mountain and to feel the feeling of freedom the word Swahili word Uhuru expresses. That freedom was a newfound value at the time and one that I continue to embody today.

After Sibusiso told us about reaching the highest peak in the world, he asked the audience this question: "Why do you think I had to climb over dead people on the way down?" The large congregation was silent, and I also paused as I thought about the horrific image he had conjured.

Were they exhausted?

Had they died of joy?

From the loss of hope?

From pure exhilaration?

From the cold?

Well, he said, "What happens—as is true in life–is that often climbers set a goal to get to the top and yet forget to set a goal to get back down to basecamp."

Climbers, or high achievers, are known for not *goal-setting through*. Think back to the last time you finished an important project. The moment it was over, did your energy plummet, and did you feel you needed a week to recover? Or have you ever set a goal to go on a holiday and then found you couldn't move for the first few days? Or have you set a goal to get married or even get a promotion, yet you did not think through the experience and envision what would come next? We lose energy when there is no goal. You hear of people retiring and then losing themselves or, worse yet, passing on. Goals are about forethought, and they are vital to our journey, our well-being and the way we lead.

In Sibusiso's story, goal setting is the process of visualizing success beyond reaching the summit, including reserving energy for getting back down the mountain. In the case of the dead climbers, it was a construct that shaped the reality of their lives and their deaths. Was the goal only to reach the top?

Is success in life when we keep striving for the top? What are we reaching for? What is success? Do we attach our worth to our performance? What if we don't reach success or the top of the mountain? What if we do but don't have the energy to get back down and enjoy the accomplishment? What if we reach success at all costs and don't have anybody to come back down to celebrate with because we have neglected the people in our lives or our other ambitions along the way?

Don't get me wrong, I love the feeling of summiting and being completely absorbed in the view from the top of a mountain; I love celebrating the achievement of reaching the top. But if I reflect on my summiting experiences, it's the execution of the journey with the people I suffered and laughed together with that fuels my long-lasting memories and emotions of fulfillment. As a former high-performance athlete, I also love the feeling of winning. It's electric when you feel the surging through you after you've given a world-class performance and then celebrate with teammates. I have played in thousands of games, travelled to many corners of the world, represented many teams, played for different leagues, and been led by different coaches, and yet truly, if you ask me what I remember the most – it's the lessons of resilience and the friendships which still stir my heart.

Sibusiso Vilane's captivating story of summiting Everest helped me understand very well from a cognitive perspective that to be successful in both mountaineering and in life, we should always think beyond achievement. And since then, I've been reminded repeatedly, to love and be grateful for the process.

Hold the vision and trust the process.

This became even more relevant when I set out on my trek up Mount Kilimanjaro with a friend. My motivation was simple: I wanted to get to the Roof of Africa (and back down) before I left the continent that had been my home for nearly seven years. I was going to continue on with my next life adventure, moving continents, and going from living in one of the smallest countries in the world to one of the largest cities.

So, that is what I set out to do, although little did I know the trip was to be so much more than *just* getting to the Roof of Africa. To be honest, I knew very little about what I was getting myself into, although I had read the story of another man who had completed the journey. We never really know what something is like until we do it. To live life is to experience it.

In the lead-up to the trip, I had done a lot of walking and hiking with a weighted bag. In retrospect, I should have done more of that and focused on leg strength and core work, although, in reality, all the conditioning in the world could not have prepared me for actually being there and pushing through the daunting conditions I ultimately faced. I did not grow up in a camping culture, so living out of a backpack or sleeping on rocks in freezing temperatures was certainly not familiar to me. Spotting rocks—ones that potentially no other hiker had seen, and which would represent a peaceful place for a pee or poo—became part of the daily mission.

For three-and-a-half days, we walked through the rain and sleet in heavy winds. We were not sleeping or bathing and I felt woozy, with a pounding headache, a sign of the start of altitude sickness. Never in my life had I imagined I'd be doing what I was doing prior to embarking upon this adventure, yet here I was, hiking out in the wilderness, putting my life in the hands of our guides. Because the weather was quite terrible, and it was hard to even see the mountain we were climbing, it became hard to remember why I was doing what I was doing or even where we were going. The blisters, the sore back, the sleep deprivation, the repetitive pea soup, and the slow and steady pole pace all started to impact my motivation. Why was I doing this again? Oh, right, to challenge me and to experience *Uhuru*, freedom, on top of the highest free-standing mountain in the world.

The Clouds Parted

And then it happened: the clouds parted and we got a glimpse of the vision, the end result. The mountain became crystal clear in that moment of blue sky, and it ignited my momentum and courage, even as the altitude sickness started to get thick, impacting my well-being and making me question my venture. That moment changed me because I was able to focus again. I was no longer distracted by the aches and the cold; I was focused on one step at a time. I remembered who I was, why I was doing this, and where we were going.

The truth is, life's like that. Having a vision is like having a destination, and the more we can crystallize it and hold on to it, the more we understand the purpose behind our daily actions through moments of challenging or good times. The same is true in our leadership work: a clear vision will create engagement. I'm especially drawn to leaders and visionaries, those who can see the unseen, what has not yet been done before. Those who are brave enough to step into the unknown. Those who have hope, who lead with a stimulating foresight. I guess, ultimately, that is what brings my forward-thinking talent to life. I love to look beyond the horizon, spend time daydreaming, and think of a future which does not yet exist anywhere except in my mind and heart. I think there's also an element of hope attached to the idea of being able to see things through. Hope is one of the greatest predictors of well-being, and when we can tap into our self-actualized selves, the feeling of hope comes to life.

> *Create a compelling vision for your future and let it fuel your calling.*

Aside from having a vision, one of the most significant parts of this mountain climbing experience was the opportunity to observe Dickson. Dickson Mbuya was our lead guide. He was perhaps a bit evasive at the first meeting while we were learning about the climb, and this caused me to question his commitment. It's funny how we can be quick to judge people. However, I was putting my life in the hands of a group of strangers, so I was still putting the cues together. On Day One of the hike, Dickson was not present. Our other much younger guide, John, took the lead in front, and there were about thirteen supporting porters with us, carrying our supplies and trailing behind. I will forever remember them as Kilimanjaro's angels.

By Day 2, I was questioning Dickson's role. He was quiet and led from the back; we learned he was not well as he was recovering from a bout of malaria. Regardless, he was there with this team. The turning point for me was when the weather soured at the same time as we began our ascent on summit night. Dickson was the first person to tell us to be prepared, to show up with all the right gear, and to pack intentionally for the fourteen-hour experience. Summit night was the peak of the experience. Although we were all emotionally and physically tired, it was the moment we had all been waiting for: the perfectly planned moment we were to make it to the top of the mountain in time for a sunrise view. Unfortunately, for some trekkers, this is the moment when they are carried back down, and we passed numerous hikers who were very ill and waiting for stretchers to hurry them back down the mountain.

The entire time we were on the ascent, I thought about the idea of goal-setting through, thinking about the two or so days it would take to descend and of course, the beach holiday awaiting me on the lustrous island of Zanzibar: my reward was rest in paradise. I had intentionally planned that trip after realizing a short bout of rest was needed before the next chapter of life was to begin.

We set out at about 1:00 a.m. When the going got tough that night, walking up the steep slopes in the pitch-black, Dickson took the lead. He paced the walk calmly. He knew when we needed rest and when to push through. His poise captivated me.

Some of our team members were struggling. Dickson remained level-headed. He was personable, he cared, and he shared stories, songs, and humour along the trail. He had demonstrated leadership by empowering his crew to take charge while he led from the back. I remember asking the third guide, the youngest of the group, what he wanted his career to be about, and without hesitation, he said he wanted to be like Dickson. Dickson is well known on Mount Kilimanjaro.

Other tour guides and groups always passed us with a big warm Mambo Jambo ("hello") to Dickson and the crew. He has ventured onto the mountain many times, spending a week every month on it, away from his family; movie producers have also hired him as a guide on movie sets. The mountain was his livelihood and he endured daily risks, though this was his gift to world explorers like me. I am honoured to have walked with him, to have learned his ways, and to admire his leadership and his humility.

Towards the summit, he encouraged me to walk ahead. "Dada (sister) Laura, you are strong. Keep going while I wait for the rest of the team," he said. And so that is how I conquered my first mountain. Full of confidence, support, and feeling cared for by a stranger, all while learning about the significance of leadership on top of the mountain. Our whole group successfully reached the summit, each spending less than ten minutes at the top and capturing the moment through photos—all while feeling a bit woozy—before rushing back down the mountain to feel better again. The descent seemed to pass in the blink of an eye, yet it involved a long trek; after nine more consecutive hours, we reached our final camping spot in the rainforest. Wow, what a feeling! I remember sharing my experience with a colleague, and she summed it up well, "if you can climb Mount Kilimanjaro, you can do anything!"

Vision is the receipt of a package that's on its way.
—*Anonymous*

You Can Do Anything!

So, while I had a personal vision to complete the hike, Dickson held the belief about creating the conditions, and *the playing field* to fulfill the vision. And even more so, Dickson as a leader demonstrated his poise and his character. This allowed his colleagues to lead the way, and to learn to take charge, so we could all get where we wanted to go. Dickson was not "performing." He was being who he was and it was admirable.

I think these are the lessons of leadership. In the workplace, we want to feel supported, cared for, and uplifted. Having the trust of leaders is empowering. When chaos or snowstorms hit— or when summiting feels daunting—these leaders take charge and continuously impart belief in a successful outcome and a vision for what is to come. They share hope. Part of the leadership quest is to know when to step up and take charge (i.e., when it's urgent or when safety is involved), and when to be present, allowing space for trial and error, and encouraging questions so learning can take place.

As a coach who helps leaders become *coach leaders*, I've learned that the key skill leaders appreciate learning about the most is how *not to* solve problems. How often, when a challenge comes up, are we quick to jump to solutions? Yet, what we know from adult learning and transformational leadership is that in the space between challenge and solution, there is a learning moment we, as leaders, need to capitalize on. As parents, coaches, and business leaders, that is the space for us to be curious, to ask questions and give space for answers to be discovered. This requires a high degree of humility as well as an understanding that we hold people capable of figuring out the answers through thinking, trial and error, and taking time for reflection and introspection. We don't learn by being told; we learn best by discovering insight through reflection or experience. This principle is also about giving the work back to the people we lead so they feel the autonomy and responsibility for committed action. What does it mean to be a *coach leader*? It means you hold the space for your people to learn, grow, and develop (more on this in Part 2).

The next time someone comes to you with a challenge (that is non-life threatening or urgent), consider staying in the challenge. You might also consider these inquiries:

- Tell me more
- If you were in my shoes, what would you suggest?
- What would success look like for this challenge?
- What's the heart of the matter here?
- How have you solved something like this in the past?

These questions, and others like them, will play a key role in helping the people you lead determine where they are going and will give them a sense of competency in getting there.

Reflect to Grow

Where Am I Going?
- Which leaders in your life have significantly impacted you?
- Which leaders do you aspire to be like?
- Which leaders have had a negative impact on your life?
- What are the lessons to consider as you shape your leadership journey?
- What vision are you moving towards?
- What are some ways you can ensure you goal-set through?
- Where in your life has your energy stopped because you haven't goal-set through?

CHAPTER 8

Agency and Vision

Leadership is to lead an intentional life that breeds internal freedom

Agency is about moving and trusting your inner world so your outer world reflects what is most important to you in the service of others. Your well-being, your satisfaction, your joy, and your performance are all counting on this internal work to generate greater fulfillment.

Whether I'm engaging with entrepreneurs, athletes transitioning out of their sport, or management professionals, most, if not all, have been navigating barriers and buying into limited beliefs. These beliefs have been instilled in them through a lifetime of experiences, societal expectations, loyalties, and pressures—some have been self-imposed limiting beliefs such as "I'm not good enough." These beliefs pop up for me, too, especially when I'm being vulnerable or going outside of my comfort zone. Having said that, turning forty-one at the time of writing this book has given me new power, something along the lines of, *well, this is how it is.* I'm now unapologetically owning my voice and watching my personal power grow. Regardless of where you are on your journey, these conscious or subconscious thoughts can disrupt us or hold us back from having a difficult conversation, asking for a promotion or stepping up into the positional power that will allow us to have the influence required of us. It is important to notice how much attention we give these voices daily.

Developing our internal power is part of our growth potential. Our inner work helps us to be clear on what beliefs are driving our thoughts, actions, and behaviours in the direction that works best for our own development and that of the people we lead.

Some people had to develop *self-assurance* growing up and learn to stand up for themselves because of their circumstances (perhaps they were bullied or had to defend themselves from a belligerent sibling, for example). Cultural norms can sometimes build a belief that it's not safe to trust other people, so children learn they must go it alone.

Yet, *self-confidence* is a synonym for self-assurance. Self-confidence is the emotional component of your personality and the most important factor in determining how you think, feel, and behave. Your level of self-confidence largely determines what you make happen in your life and gives you the power to make choices that will benefit you and the people with whom you engage.

Key elements of self-confidence:
- the degree to which you evaluate yourself as competent (generally, rather than in terms of a specific skill)
- your internal dialogue (affirming the good in who you are, your values and beliefs, how much you like yourself, and how much you trust your abilities)
- and outwardly, the skills you have acquired and the committed practice you have invested in developing them

Self-confidence, coupled with the power of self-image, allows you to outwardly act in a way that is consistently aligned with your internal view of yourself. *If you like yourself, you'll set higher standards, strive to reach bigger goals and persist for longer in achieving those goals.*[20]

Self-confidence can be found and applied to many different elements of your life; it allows you to be bold, take risks, ask for that promotion, win an interview, have difficult conversations, set boundaries, and so forth. Picture a lioness striding through the animal kingdom. She doesn't need to profess that she is a lion; she just is. And that is the start of building your personal power.

Here are some other things to think about when building your personal power:

- Do an honest assessment of your internal locus of control: who are you being accountable to and who are you giving power to regarding your actions and your life? If you are waiting for other people, then you're giving up your power. If you own that control or power, then it's your responsibility to make things happen.
- Ask yourself what you want for your life, as in the *Grand Vision* exercise below. Set challenging "stretch" goals: focus on your strengths and values so you stay true to yourself, then be optimistic in pursuit of what is to come. Visualize the outcome that you want to move towards, surround yourself with people who will lift you and reach out for help if you get stuck!
- Try to accept feelings and suspend judgment. Let go of the idea that you need the approval of others to be accepted. You are enough. Develop an attitude of gratitude towards yourself.
- Be aware of comparison misleading your efforts—it is the thief of joy. Be intentional with your use of social media; it probably has a bigger impact on you than you think.

Current Reality to Vision: When you realize agency, you can access the power of vision

> *As you start to walk on, the way appears.*
> *—Rumi*

Vision, like purpose, provides direction and can create meaning in your life. It is a gift to be able to imagine. Having a vision creates a mental image that inspires you to reflect, grow and turn dreams into reality. Visions are valuable because they are products of the mind and heart; they integrate our sense of purpose and values with the picture of how to accomplish what we want.

Have you considered your Big Hairy Audacious Goals "BHAGS," as author and business consultant Jim Collins calls them?[21] At work, amongst your peers, managers, or teams, or at home, amongst your friends and family members, what do people need to see and believe in, especially when you're in the weeds of "the doing of daily tasks." Knowing the direction and the current strategic priorities will help your people connect the dots between their current reality and the vision.

There's one great truth you can count on whoever you are and whatever you do: when you really want something, that desire originated from the soul of the universe. The universe then conspires to help you move towards it. This is also the practice of agency and leading from within.

Are you curious enough to develop a vision for yourself, your family, or your team? Having a vision is like perfume for the mind. Without vision, without dreams, we can get caught up in what *has been* instead of moving towards what *can be*. A vision adds power to your sense of agency and means your everyday actions can move you closer to being the person you want to be.

A Grand Vision

1. **Health and Fitness.** What health goals do you have for yourself? What are your physical ambitions?
2. **Intellectual Life.** How much are you learning, growing and expanding your mind and your thoughts? What courses, conferences, or discussions would challenge you?
3. **Emotional Life.** How are you intentionally developing your emotional capacities? What about your muscles of resiliency and empathy?
4. **Character.** What values do you want to embody in your life? Your career? Your aspirations?
5. **Spiritual Life.** What would a spiritual life look like for you? What practices allow you to connect, meditate, pray and journal? What difference would these make for your being?
6. **Primary Relationships.** Who do you spend time with and how do you make each other feel?
7. **Parenting or Caregiving.** What do you value when it comes to raising children? How do you spend time with your kids? What are the personality traits that support you in this?
8. **Social Life.** Who are your friends? How much time do you want to spend with them? What do your weekends look like? How many friends are close/personal? Does that suit you?
9. **Financial Life.** What are your goals in terms of saving, lifestyle, investments, etc.? What assets do you want to

own? How much income do you want to earn (passively and in terms of salary)? How much cash do you desire? What about liquidity assets?
10. **Career.** What do you want to do? Is your job part of your mission? At what level do you want to work? Do you want to be world-class at what you do? How much time do you want your career to take up?
11. **Quality of Life.** What do you want your surroundings to be like? What kind of environment for your home and workplace do you desire?
12. **Life Vision.** What mark do you want to leave on the world?

"Wow," you might think, "there is a lot to consider here." Be gentle with yourself. Out of the above list, what's most important to you right now, in this current season? Intention and attention are at the heart of human development; focus on what you are giving intention to and what needs more of your attention? Try to rank these from 1-10 to get a snapshot of your current reality. Select a few areas that stand out and that you can celebrate. Notice if there are any areas that need even more of your attention. What intentions do you want to set around those specific areas?

Now, take this a step further. Envision a few different scenarios and a timeline for the coming weeks, months or years—however far out you can see yourself as you practice this visioning exercise. Take time to draw out some possibilities. How do you want your life to go? Where do you want to be? What do you want to be doing? Who do you want to become? Gather thoughts, pictures and emotions about what pulls you. Carve out some time to create a vision board with your ideal world. Let your identity, purpose, and values fuel your vision. And enjoy the ride!

There is great power in manifestation. I remember when I first started learning about the power of goal setting and visualization. My life started to move in different ways than ever before. Taking inventory of my current reality (especially my finances) evoked a rude awakening. I then started setting some specific goals and that area of my life started to evolve. At one point, I told a friend I didn't want to vision anymore because my life was moving so quickly. I was afraid that if I set more goals, they were going to become reality! What an incredible place to be! Have the courage to dream. If we don't dream, how else can we create a future that does not yet exist?

Make time for visions, since you move towards what you think about. Keep them as your most dominant thoughts and then let the process unfold. Add emotion to your visions; we are moved by the emotion of an experience, more than simply a thought of it. And remember to reverse engineer each of your visions. What first action can you take to move one step closer to them? What processes and accountabilities do you need to put in place so you can step into living your best life?

Over the last few years, I have been facilitating a women's retreat called Fall Forward. This intimate workshop has included a visioning exercise and a meditation. The results have been astounding. Several participants recently contacted me to share how their year had evolved, from career pivots to relationship goals and health and travel aspirations. Much had come true already, and a lot was still in motion. Part of visioning involves letting things be. Plant the seed of what you desire in your subconscious mind; it may need some watering once in a while, but trust that it's there and in the process of coming to fruition. Sometimes, we can't see the growth – like when you plant seeds in a flower bed, yet you know that by creating the conditions with a bit more watering and letting Mother Nature play her part, beauty arises. If I leave you with one experienced practice of self-leadership, it's to be intentional about your forethought and *goal-set through* so you can continue to maximize your evolution in the areas of your life that are most relevant to you.

The consequences of not being intentional are that we can live a life of waiting, hoping, wishing, or, worse yet, blaming, deflecting, and neglecting ourselves.

Like many other people, I grew up always waiting for the next "step" to unlock. When can I start going out alone? When can I start driving a car? When can I travel without my family? When can I have my own bank account? When can I finish school? And so on. But when we entered our adult life, many of us went into stagnation mode. Yes, we chose something—a job, a partner, a life. But we also started waiting. And often, nothing came to us anymore. And the longer we spent in this state, the more scared we became of choosing differently and changing our situation. And we kept waiting.

When things are more stable. When I have more money. When the kids are older. When x, y, and z happen, *then* I will…

It's human and it's also a trap. There is no security and there will never be. There is never the right moment to do something. The only choice available is whether you want to *live* your life intentionally with agency or wait it away. Both choices are there for you. Go ahead and select the comfortable life of "I will change when…" But be aware that you are telling yourself a lie. To live life, you have to choose to do so despite the consequences and things that are not perfect yet. Because, really, we can only open our eyes so many times. Talk to elderly people and ask them how fast life passes. If you want to explore the depths of the courage tank at your disposal in choosing life, continue to follow me on my journey.

As with a lush garden in full bloom, part of living an intentional life is also about setting up the conditions for you and others to thrive. While this might be the most difficult part of the experience, when we do start to make intentional choices about what is important for us (first on the inside)—so the people around us can be drawn to our inspired life—then we also want to set up the playing field and conditions for our ultimate fulfillment – to positively contribute to others' well-being and success. This is what we will explore in Part 2, creating the conditions and cultures for a thriving ecosystem and illustrating that our inner works create the world on the outside.

There is a careful, honourable science behind reprogramming our brains through the education and applied practice of neuroplasticity; anyone can benefit from it.[22] In fact, perhaps you might wonder how this might benefit you and your team, organization, or family.

Without this conscious leadership of self, we have no awareness to allow us to unlock, unleash, or fully explore all that sits inside of us or the people with whom we engage daily. By contrast, to live by intent and to make leadership choices that align with who we are and who we want to become, we must make choices that leave a lasting impact on ourselves, our family, our community, our nation, and even our world. It is time to go deep. Because here is what is at the heart of authentic leadership: knowing who you are, why you exist, and where you are going is the start of the journey. I hope you find peace, gentleness, and excitement as you continue to move forward in exercising your leadership for the greater good. Your agency is about doing the inner work, having clarity on your world while holding compassion for your actions on the lives of others.

We always almost have a choice - at least around how we respond to the things that happen to us. (I recognize that this is easier said than done, especially when deep-rooted thoughts, emotions, and activators can flare repeatedly when under pressure). What are you currently moving away from? And what are you moving towards? The moments of small everyday decisions—or even life-changing decisions—are expressed in the way we lead our complex inner worlds.

Deciding to play in this space of conscious authentic leadership gives birth to the *self-discovery journey* so your everyday decisions and actions move you and your teams, organizations, families, and communities towards greater sustained performance and well-being. It assists you to live the life you desire and helps you create the positive impact you want so you can enjoy a fulfilled, meaningful existence.

PART 2
To WE

ENGAGING OTHERS

PART 2 INTRODUCTION: ENGAGING OTHERS

The significance of relationships and working with others is part of our humanness.

So far, most of the leadership reflections in this book have been about leading the self and exploring the system within. The following chapters explore the important shift of working with others, and the complexities that lie within bringing people together in a healthy and productive manner. The transition from focusing on "Me" to embracing the inclusive "We" involves applying the insights you've learned about yourself in Part 1 (self-discovery) to your interactions with people, teams, relationships, and others within a specific ecosystem.

The conversation shifts:

From	To
Who Am I?	Who Are WE?
Why Do I Exist?	Why Do WE Exist?
Where Am I Going?	Where are WE Going?

While personal leadership work is important for our individual lives, it is amplified when we are in a position to lead others. How we then lead and engage others has a significant impact on whether they disengage or thrive within their workplace ecosystem. What we are explicitly talking about here are the ways in which we communicate and work together in the workplace: relationship management, aligning talent with purpose, working in teams, and so forth. When people work, business works.

According to Gallup, approximately seventy percent of the variance in employee engagement can be attributed to the quality of an employee's manager. In other words, managers have a significant impact on employee and team-level engagement. In fact, leadership is the single most important factor in whether or not an employee thrives in their workplace[23]. The cost of disengagement is enormous. Recent (2023) global engagement trends see twenty-three percent of the global workforce identify as being engaged in their world; fifty-nine percent of the global workforce are not engaged (otherwise known as the quiet quitters) and eighteen percent are actively disengaged. Moreover, low engagement costs the global economy $8,800,000,000 dollars or nine percent of global GDP[24]. There is immense value in knowing how best to lead and engage others, and this is probably the most difficult task we face.

Part 2 intently outlines solutions to countering disengagement by offering the managerial and human skills to move people from surviving to thriving. This is the part of leadership that excites me the most: how we show up and create conditions for other people to thrive. Leading, then, becomes about exploring the ecosystem we function within (excluding technological and political realms) and how to behave so we work together towards a common goal.

If you are in a position of authority or influence in your work, community, or personal life, then Part 2 is written for you. We will explore the impact your leadership has on the people around you as you build a world-class, strengths-based team, organization, family, or community. You will learn about the Playing Field, the Ways of Working together and your approach to realizing what leadership looks and feels like when you unlock the full potential of performance.

For me, coming from a high-performance team sports background, there is an obvious realization: great work and great performance cannot be done alone. People are designed for connection, belonging, sharing, and collaborating, as the old African Proverb beautifully states,

> *If you want to go fast go alone, if you want to go far, go together.*
> *– African Proverb*

CHAPTER 9

The Playing Field

Leadership creates space for creativity to unlock

I like to think of the *Playing Field* as an arena that gives you clarity around which game you're playing, a clear understanding of why you're playing, where you're going with the game, who you are becoming as a player, and what leadership skills are required to play the game effectively and in collaboration with others. When you become aware of all the arenas in which you get to play—work, life, or sport—you are choosing the conditions of the playing field and creating a clear understanding of what you will allow to impact your way of being or performance as a team. The conditions are about naming how you will engage and not engage with each other, the approaches in your leadership style so it is conducive to the environment in which you are participating, and other important human skills to maximize team or group effectiveness.

Setting Up the Playing Field

Imagine a soccer (football) field, either a grand stadium like FC Barcelona with seating for 100,000 fans or your neighbourhood park where young kids are shuffling along, learning to pass the ball between cones. The playing field has boundaries on either side; these boundaries represent your values or principles that govern how you will behave. When is the ball inbounds and when is it out of bounds? What behaviours tell you when you are inbounds and which ones tell you or your colleagues or teammates when you are out of bounds?

Our behaviours are tangible and visible actions that inform our value system. Only when you know the answers to those questions can you be true to yourself and play the game you want to play which in turn directs the way you want to lead for the greater good.

Authenticity lives in the space of staying true to your values system that informs the conditions of play. This becomes particularly important as our values get tested the most when we are under pressure, for example when dealing with the pressures of decision-making, especially as it relates to issues that will elevate or cause harm to yourself, your team, your family, or your organization.

To build on this metaphor of the arena, for the game to continue to be played, the ball needs to stay in bounds. There are goalposts at each end of the field, and a referee will toss a coin toss to determine which end your team must protect and which end is yours to score on. There are eleven players on the playing field at a time and your team is supplemented by substitute players who are ready to jump in, as well as a manager and some support staff. Sometimes there are lots of people in the stands, sometimes not so many. Some days, it pours rain. Other days, the blistering sun shines down on you. Regardless, you must always be ready to play. When it comes to game day, the intention is clear: show up, warm up, strategize, do your best, help the team win, cool down, celebrate and reflect, and then carry on with your day. Just like that, the game is played.

Except there's so much more to the game. Setting up the playing field in sports, as well as in the playing fields of work, family, and other areas of life, is intricate. It's messy. We are complex human beings before we are human *doings,* and I think that's what we can forget in sports, in the workplace, and in life generally. Now, let's take this a step further to set up the conditions of a team, an environment, or an ecosystem; these conditions allow you to then create the playing field for performance and well-being to thrive.

There is a slight difference between a *group* or *team* of people coming together engaging in a working relationship; whatever playing field you are creating, choose to explore. A team has a clear and compelling performance challenge with a common purpose that they are moving towards. A team is made up of individuals who work interdependently with each other and rely on each other to get work done collaboratively (as opposed to a group of individuals who dependently work on their own tasks). In a team, we have clear and explicit norms such as agreed-upon behaviours; there is mutual accountability. Trust is critical so that healthy conflict can take place and individuals are safe to share their expression of truth or opinion to contribute to the greater good of their team's goal.

So, to set up the Playing Field, we must first understand that individuals are uniquely wired, as we discovered in our discussion of strengths and talents in Part 1. The same uniqueness also applies to groups of people, cultures, teams, and organizations. Ideal leaders, and ideal teams, have common characteristics, the most important of which is that unique ways of being are celebrated and included, and space is created for unique beings to shine in different settings.

Part of setting up our Playing Field requires us to lay out the groundwork:

- Who are we?
- Why do we exist?
- Where are we going?
- How will we behave?
- Who does what and by when?

Once the basics are understood, we can build a strategy for who does what and by when. I often meet with teams that started with their strategic meetings only to realize months later that they need to integrate cultural elements into their strategy. If your people are not at the forefront of your strategy, then how will it be executed? We need to start at the place of understanding who we are as team members before we build purpose and mission. Performance, collaboration, and effectiveness will follow.

I have heard repeatedly that engaging in team-building and, more intentionally, also in team coaching, is necessary for sustained engagement. Through interactive strengths-based team conversations, and several other team effectiveness modalities, my clients have valued and prioritized team-based development as part of their people strategy to ensure maximum performance and well-being.

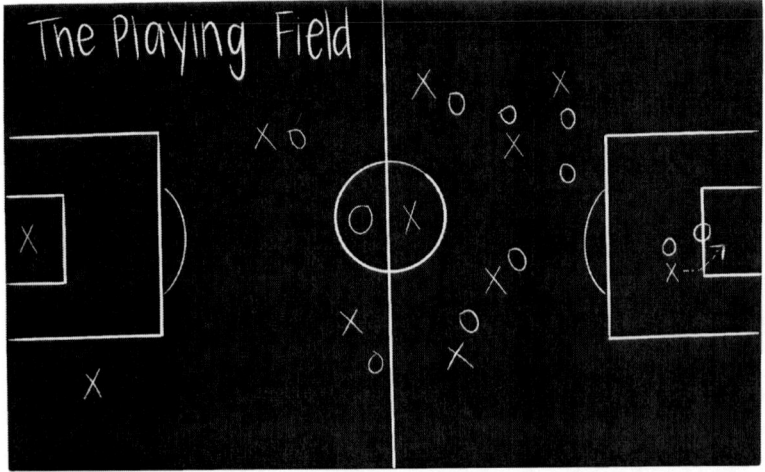

The Playing Field

The Playing Field
1. **Talent: Who are we?**
   When individuals come together and are recognized for their unique strengths and weaknesses, we learn that we are better together and that we cannot succeed on our own. Identifying talent— including what skills, attributes, and natural ways of thinking each team member can contribute—is essential to building a team. When we focus on our needs and strengths, we start to build language around who we are as people. Once we know who is in the room, then we can move to identify a clear and specific common purpose that adds value to the stakeholders you serve.

   - Take stock of unique individual skills/interests/strengths.
   - What skills do we have on our team? What do others count on us for?
   - What skills do we need to learn/further develop to support your team?
   - What do you want others to know about you that hasn't yet been expressed?

2. **Purpose: Why do We Exist?**
   Why are we here? What is our common purpose? Success means knowing we have contributed to improving a mission or cause that supports the greater good. A company may have a purpose statement and, equally important, a department or team may have a specific common purpose that feeds into the larger organizational purpose. Clarity is important here, as purpose becomes the anchor when challenges arise.

- Why do you exist as a team? As a department? As an organization?
- Who does your team create value for?
- Without your team, what would be missing from your organization and the way in which you add value to your stakeholders?
- Without your organization, what would be missing from society?
- Think of moments or highlights in the last year where your team positively contributed to people's lives. What did you generate for others as a result of your team's actions?
- How might this change in the coming years?

3. **Values: How will we behave?**

   Our ways of behaving speak the truth of our values. Just like the sidelines of a soccer field, our values indicate which behaviours are acceptable and which are not. When values are clear, behaviours are clear, which can accelerate performance or give permission to course-correct when behaviours are "out-of-bounds." Similar to a policy or a list of rules-of-engagement, they exist to ensure mutual accountability regarding performance behaviours that are celebrated and respected. Chapter 10, *Ways of Working,* expands on this concept.

   - What do you like and value about the way your team currently behaves? What values do you demonstrate through these behaviours?
   - Equally important, what don't you like about the way this team currently behaves? What values are being compromised when we don't behave in a more productive way?

- From your *Ways of Working*, we can identify and embody our values as a team and organization. How will we behave in pursuit of our purpose and goals? If we behave in such a way that models our values, what can stop us?

4. **Vision: Where are we going?**
Setting a vision is similar to goal setting in that it generates energy. As discussed in Part 1, when we have clarity around what we're moving towards, we unlock creative energy within team members to contribute and participate. Without a goal, we won't know where to focus our attention—and where we focus our intention, is where we give our energy.

- What outcome goals do we want to achieve in the coming period? What will success look like? How will we measure success?
- What process goals will help us along the way? What short-term goals can we focus on, the incremental goals, that will help us achieve our outcome goals?

5. **Strategy: What are our tactics?**
Coming up with a game plan (who does what and by when) is part of setting up the conditions of the playing field and moves us from talking to action. Action must follow so that progress can be celebrated. When there is no action, perhaps expectations are not clear and may need to be revisited. Only when we have clear expectations of strategy can we move towards healthy feedback, accountability and team success.

- What are our priorities for this time?
- Who needs to do what and by when?

- How will we keep each other accountable?
- What can get in the way?
- What is the first action we need to take?

The Playing Field
Reflect on the current conditions of your team's playing field. Which area might you want to be more intentional about to set everyone up for success?

CHAPTER 10

Ways of Working

Leadership is both an art and a science

Whether you're a new team lead, have a new team forming, or want better working relationships, the concepts we address in this chapter will set you up for success. We know that individually we have different working preferences: people get along with some of them naturally, and others are more difficult to deal with. An important reason why team leaders call upon my team facilitation skills is to bring clarity to their agreed-upon *Ways of Working*.

The benefit of this practical exercise is that it names values and brings them to life by discussing ways of behaving that support doing good work together and leaning into difficult conversations when needed. Team members will share vulnerable feelings with me about feeling unseen, disrespected, shamed, and more, in professional work settings. The cost to the organization is disengagement, conflict among team members, unmotivated staff, and what we know as quiet quitters. On the flip side, the alignment and energy that is evoked by activating agreed-upon Ways of Working has left participants feeling seen, heard, celebrated, encouraged, and ready to take on the work at hand. The co-creation process here is important in ensuring each team member feels a part of the established team norms, which in turn creates co-accountability.

The way your people engage with one another can foster a healthy team culture. An example of an agreed upon way of working would be the way meetings are held: has it been agreed that they will all have a clear purpose, process, and actionable outcome with accountability? If you have weekly meetings, and people don't feel energized into action following them, plus there's no accountability on the action items, then how productive are these meetings truly?

As a leader, if you are hesitating about discussing performance issues, there may be some underlying beliefs that are holding you back (for example, maybe you don't want to upset someone). However, a co-created team framework will give team members and managers permission to have difficult conversations by putting the work at the centre of the conversation and using agreed-upon *Ways of Working* as anchors in the process.

Diagnosing the health of your team is more obvious at some points than at others. Some of my clients have been baffled by high turnover, low productivity, and lack of effort and motivation, all traceable to the health of their team. With a developmental tool such as the Team BluePrint™, you can gain a visual representation of your current team culture. A tool like this allows you to pinpoint which shared beliefs and values impact the performance of your team. It is helpful to identify common team dysfunctions, such as a lack of trust, difficulty navigating conflict, a lack of accountability, or lack of results themselves. With any developmental tool, it's important to establish tangible actions for moving forward so that the culture continues to grow in the most productive way. *Ways of Working* simply come down to how we engage with each other, communicate, celebrate, acknowledge, and keep each other accountable to the work at hand.

Walking the talk is, of course, easier said than done. Yet, this is what differentiates the leaders and organizations that are brave enough to do daring human-centred work. *Ways of Working* starts with identifying values and acting on those values: they are like the boundaries of play; the boundaries of which behaviours are acceptable and which are not. Establishing collective *Ways of Working* allows us to build mutual accountability and hold each other to certain performance standards. Behaviours demonstrate the preferred way of engaging with each other and give team members permission to act on consequences, be it for celebrating agreed-upon behaviour or leaning into course-correcting behaviour, otherwise known as feedback. How we engage with one another, and lead others, says more about our character than our personality. When the desired behaviours are clearly articulated and collectively discussed, clarity ensues in the hearts and minds of those participating on the playing field together. What is required here is a safe space to explore what is and is not working so it can be highly beneficial to have a facilitator to guide the process.

> ***Behaviour is the mirror in which everyone shows their image.***

I've actively provided leadership consulting and coaching for the last several years to a tech start-up that experienced a rapid growth phase which required the leadership team (not just the CEO) to work through operationalizing their values. The benefit of this ongoing exercise was that it gave clarity to staff and managers in calling out performance errors, giving detailed feedback, and maintaining consistent behaviour; this was extended to client services and the work at the centre of the conversation. Initially, during our engagements, the CEO was the one who stated the company's values. However, as the leadership team grew and more departments and sub-teams were created, the conversation became a company-wide opportunity to build and agree upon the lived values. The conversations about crystalizing what values looked like in action—expressed through behaviours—became more important as more employees joined the company. It's important to let your *Ways of Working* evolve. People are not static; just as we grow and evolve, so do our *Ways of Working* with one another. Carving out intentional time to bring clarity to these behaviours is part of setting up your playing field.

In large companies, spending time discussing *Ways of Working* within departments and teams has its own benefits. We usually see values expressed somewhere on a company website or on a physical sign at the entry to a corporate head office. However, the operationalizing of values takes place within teams, within the parameters of a working group that works together day in and day out. There is a difference between aspiring to live out organization-wide values and living them within a smaller unit of working relationships. This practice of articulating your *Ways of Working* is important so that you can create a culture within the larger culture of the company and get to know how best to work with one another on a daily basis.

Making Hard Decisions

Leaders sometimes need to make hard decisions about behaviour; and, when these decisions are clearly expressed, they serve to protect all involved. The idea of agreed-upon team values and norms goes beyond organizational policies and codes of conduct; it speaks to how people know to behave in the team environment so performance and well-being can thrive. The tricky part is that people change and grow, as do teams. They evolve. The optimal time to revisit established Ways of Working and discuss, edit, and adjust as needed is when people leave or are moved to a new position, or when new team members are onboarded.

We see conflict avoidance as a breeding ground for quiet quitting, disengagement, and toxic behaviours to take root. Conflict avoided is conflict multiplied. When new teams are formed, or conflict arises on an existing team, a shared language is required to invoke alignment. When we as leaders can hold space to ask open-ended questions, and give time to the unseen values that are driving people's behaviours, performance will accelerate. Think of it as slowing down to speed up. Imagine all the time it takes to prepare to give and receive feedback, the discretionary energy it takes to work through the emotional and psychological weight of calling out behaviours that are taking away from the work at hand. Instead, you can simplify the process by taking time to pause, discuss and align. In leadership and teamwork, you want to make sure that you have shared definitions of the values that drive behaviours and shape culture so work can be completed together as peers towards a common goal.

Leadership is responsible for creating the culture in the workplace ecosystem. If we don't intentionally put energy into building cultures, cultures will develop autonomously and may evolve in many different directions. Habits, attitudes, and mindsets start to take over, and the company or team culture can turn from "team success" to "individual success." Toxicity can easily begin to infuse the culture, blurring the boundary between acceptable and unacceptable behaviour. It takes deliberate, intentional practice to build healthy environments where people feel safe and supported, and it's our role as leaders to set the parameters for a discussion of culture that is at the forefront of our strategy and execution.

Investing in Success

It has long been recognized that investing in people and culture has a direct impact on a company's success. It can improve morale and engagement, facilitate adaptation to change related to personnel and technology, and enhance performance metrics, client satisfaction, and gross profit[25]. Culture is about the collective thinking and behaviour of your people. Culture is everyone's responsibility, including, and perhaps most importantly, that of people in positions of authority. Part of that responsibility is to be mindful and intentional about the group dynamics in order to keep tabs on whether the culture is veering off track, moving from healthy and productive to nonadaptive and constraining. Spending time on your Ways of Working is about creating the conditions for people to develop, thrive and be engaged in meaningful work. I have seen first-hand that investing time to slow down and facilitate team discussions results in meaningful engagements for people and teams to not only come together but to know one another, to be seen, and to have the energy to complete the work at hand. In addition, knowing how to navigate difficult conversations helps people keep each other committed and accountable to the work at hand. Culture matters. It makes everyone matter.

Company culture is about more than proclaiming your values on your website.

✘ **Culture is not:**

>Motivational posters
>A pizza party
>T-shirts with a company logo
>Ping pong during lunch
>Benefits and vacation days

☑ **Culture is:**

- Shared and embodied beliefs and values
- How you hire talent and let people go
- How people get promoted and/or developed
- How you navigate conflict
- What stories are told and retold
- Whether you feel safe to speak up

Whether you seek to cultivate one or not, your organization's culture already exists. It's the reason why people stay and why people go. The question is: does your culture help people belong and perform collectively with a proven belief that they matter?

To provide an environment for culture to thrive, consider:

1. Beliefs: What will your people stand for?
2. Behaviours: How should people act when no one is looking?
3. Stories: What stories will showcase shared beliefs?
4. Traditions: How do you come together in a meaningful way?
5. Artifacts: What is a physical expression of your culture?
6. Systems: What can make it easier to live what you speak?

Don't wait until your employees are out the door. Be intentional about cultivating a culture where people want to belong.

Ways of Working Activity

Note: This exercise can be completed in reflection as a leader or among teammates. Sit with your team as a whole and answer these questions together.

1. In our team/organization, when do we need to find our values? When is it hard? When does it work?
2. What do we like and value about the way this team works?
3. What don't we like or value about the way this team works?
4. What values are we trying to express through our behaviours?
5. What are the shared definitions of our top two or three values?
6. What are we missing?
7. What can we do better?
8. What is one thing you can do to help grow the culture?
9. How will we hold each other accountable for our *Ways of Working* and engage with each other?
10. What are the consequences when we are out of bounds?

CHAPTER 11
People Leadership Skills

Leadership requires radical empathy

It's one thing to set up the Playing Field conditions, but it's the day-to-day interactions that sustain working relationships in a meaningful and productive way. As a leader, you need to be intentional in your approach and develop your relationship skills to best engage others. Relationship skills matter in every part of life but they are most significant if you're in a position of authority. We know this through research; we know this through experience. The work here for you as the leader is to invest in the skills I refer to as the *Coach-Approach*, an inquiry-based style of coaching. Weaving the *Coach-Approach* into your leadership practice maximizes your ability to create a culture built on trust and care, and ensure your team's relational needs are met. Team members need to feel a sense of belonging and they need to feel safe, connected, and validated. In combination with meeting these relational needs, you need to keep people in the learning zone so they can thrive on a performance and human level. Practicing these skills will result in greater engagement, creativity, and productivity and overall increase in your team's sense of well-being. The interesting part is that when we put these skills into practice, we are both exuding care and accountability. Sounds simple, *right?*

Building effective relationships is part of your everyday leadership practice. It requires intentionality and this happens over time. This is not about being best friends with everyone around you; it is about building authentic connections so work can thrive in a container of "togetherness and safety." If you are curious about your relationship-building effectiveness and want to know your areas of strength or opportunities to develop, the Emotional Capital Report™ can shed light on the key attributes that will enhance the vital practice of connecting.[26] For example, being relentlessly curious about your own leadership and then extending that curiosity to others confirms that you want to learn and are genuinely interested in the development and performance of those you lead. Curiosity brings people closer. Asking meaningful questions or giving feedback requires a degree of straightforwardness in your approach, which is rooted in your own self-confidence.

This chapter offers practical skills and activities to develop your leadership relational skills. You will explore why some questions are more powerful than others and what it means to truly listen. The people skills required within the *Coach-Approach* may challenge your desire to "fix" or give advice and require you to adopt other ways of coaching and mentoring your people. Yes, there's a time and place for quick advice and solutions. However, the most transformational encounters require leaders to hold space, enquire more deeply, and allow the person you're talking with to come up with their own creative way forward.

Here are some people-related leadership skills that will set you up for success:

1. Listen more, talk less
2. Stay present-future focused
3. Understand people's strengths and needs

4. Stay curious and open-minded
5. Remember that you don't need to know all the answers

The Coach-Approach

Since the level of employee and team engagement depends a great deal upon their managers, managers now more than ever need to become coach leaders. The *Coach-Approach* helps employees identify their talents and have meaningful and inspiring career and performance conversations with their leaders.

Listening for Needs: Activate the Third Ear

The greatest tool of all might be listening for needs.

It sounds so simple: ask questions and listen intently. Check in on this though: are you listening to respond? Are you listening so you can give advice and consult on what you think to be true? Or are you listening to what the other person is *not* saying? Are you truly engaged in picking up on the narrative, the context, and the emotions of the person you are speaking with? This approach is what I call listening with our *Third Ear.* We, as managers, leaders, coaches, and employers, need to activate our *Third Ear* to listen holistically to what people are saying and not saying.

Activating the *Third Ear* takes practice. Learning to be present so people feel fully seen is a lifelong skill; it's one that requires you to appreciate another's perspective, story, or idea, and to see it as providing added value. As people, leaders ideally demonstrate the skill of being present in our own selves before we engage in another person's story. *Listening is not about you as the leader, it's about the other person.*

Take a moment and think of a time when you felt really heard. Recall when someone listened to you and heard what *was really important to you on the deepest level. What was this experience like? How did it make you feel?*

Listening and being listened to with full presence can be awe-inspiring and can drastically improve the quality of our relationships as well as our performance. As I have been reflecting on my leadership coaching journey, I've noticed coaching isn't something I turn on and off anymore. It's become my way of engaging in conversation. The *Coach-Approach* is a way of life that connects me to people through deep and meaningful reflections and conversations. I have become a committed listener, both as a person and as a professional. For example, in my friendships, I notice what people are not saying and dare to ask additional questions to help people discover what they might not be seeing. In my coaching relationships, I take note of small, subtle changes in a client's tone of voice or a shift in their energy and tap into an intuitive sense that there could be *more*.

A powerful way to access this space is by understanding and applying the Levels of Listening:

Level 1: You are quick to respond from your ego—the experience is about you, not the other person
Level 2: You provide a non-judgemental presence and can explore positive intention
Level 3: You listen for needs and values

Level 1 listening is when we simply listen to the content of the story, and we find ourselves automatically responding according to our internal dialogue. At this level, we may even make a quick judgement—positive or negative—about the person who is talking. We spend a lot of time as a culture in Level 1 listening and, as a result, we aren't truly hearing the person with whom we are engaging.

Level 2 listening requires us to be centred and to withhold judgement and our immediate responses in order to stay focused on attentively listening to the person who is speaking. This active listening creates a deeper place of care and rapport and opens up space for deeper conversations.

Level 3 listening—or activating your *Third Ear*—goes beyond the words that are spoken. You are as present as one can be with someone else, moving beyond language and holding space for the context of what the other person is describing. This type of listening requires a higher degree of emotional awareness wherein we give space and attention to the subtle body gestures, tones, energy, and emotion behind the other person's words. We are present and hold space for the needs and values the other person is truly trying to express.

One way to be more present is to slow down: to ask, pause, listen, and lead in a state of continuous curiosity. As you listen, pause to hold space for a few seconds more than you think is necessary. When you give people time and space to process and think, you start to help them unlock what is in their conscious mind and assist them to access their creativity and agency so they can come up with new realizations themselves. *It's our role as leaders and coaches to show up believing in people's capabilities and to remain present to help them realize their potential.*

Strengths/Needs Paradigm

Let's think about the complexity of the systems that exist between people. As mentioned, if only one in 33,000,000 people share your personal thinking pattern (according to the Gallup CliftonStrengths™), imagine what it's like to work with another person who also has a thinking pattern that is as rare as one in 33,000,000. You've probably experienced this! Let's say you have a gut feeling about an important decision that needs to be made, and the other person you are speaking with just cannot relate to your "gut;" they need data, facts, and logic instead. Their truth is different from your truth. As a result, the space between you will seem vast, a contrast to how things seem when you recognize you are leading from different places of talent.

There are things you know about yourself, such as how you think, act, and behave when you're at your best, and the same goes for those you work with. There are also unknown areas of your leadership style that come out when you're under pressure. The key is to be curious about your strengths and weaknesses, as well as about the needs you have as a people leader. Likewise, it's important to know your team members' unique contributions, needs, and values so you can be intentional with how you engage them. When you demonstrate genuine care and curiosity about leveraging and celebrating your people's strengths, and provide space for their needs to be met, you are well on your way to leading with excellence. Focusing on strengths versus dwelling on weaknesses is a sure-fire way to move towards success and the well-being of your team.

You may ask your team members to complete their Gallup CliftonStrengths™ assessments so you (and they) can also learn about their needs. For example, a person with a strong need for learning and development will crave growth-based challenges. If their need for growth is not being met, they might feel disengaged and start looking elsewhere for a new challenge. A person with strong relational needs might benefit greatly from some additional time for one-on-one connection. A common discovery in team engagement workshops is that members don't know their fellow team members and are missing the authentic connection that allows trust to form. Alternatively, one person might value a detailed process, while another wants autonomy in the way in which they get their work done. Strengths and needs are never linear but increasing self-awareness through assessment tools supports one's understanding.

Needs Are Not Linear

In the realm of workplace well-being and the degree to which we, as individual contributors and team members, can perform at our best over a sustained period, an intentional commitment to understanding needs is required. Each individual will have a unique expectation of what their career means for them—and what they need to sustain their performance and well-being journey. To illustrate this further, in their studies of reimagining Maslow's Hierarchy of Needs in the modern workplace, the Maslow Research Center came to understand that we have layers of needs[27]:

- **Basic needs,** such as a positive onboarding experience, job safety, well-being and inclusivity
- **Relational needs**, such as belonging and positive interactions with peers
- **Growth needs,** which include leadership role modelling, purpose broadcasting, clear goal setting, having a coach leader to challenge them and help them grow in their professional development, and so forth.

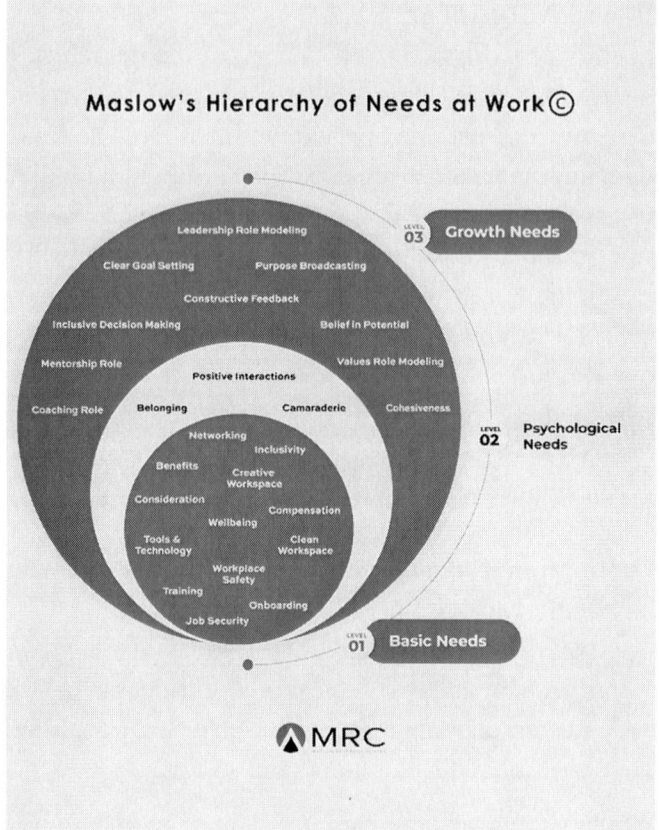

Maslow Hierarchy of Needs at Work

The strengths that comprise a functioning team may also point the way to their needs. For example, a team that is dominant in what the CliftonStrengths™ labels "relationship building" will have a stronger culture of belonging, connection, and friendship than a team that values strategic thinking or pure execution. This is the nonlinear aspect of building culture; since each person is uniquely wired, each team and organization will move through different phases to meet the individual and collective needs of the people in it. Organizational structures can play a pivotal role in the way people interact with each other and the way leaders engage others. For example, when lines of communication are limited by job design.

It's up to us to be curious about the needs of the whole person as they live, work, and perform. The first step towards better understanding human needs and developing strategies and language that help ensure those needs are met, is to identify the needs that will allow us as leaders to move to a thriving organization. This can happen at the individual, team, and organizational levels.

Unmet Needs

One female executive client recently shared with me their frustration about not being seen in the boardroom in a male-dominant setting, not so much in the physical sense but in the sense that they did not feel their opinion was sought or heard. The situation was compounded by the fact that the meeting was held remotely over Zoom. The truth is, all people, leaders, teams, and organizations have blind spots, points of pain you can't see yet which definitely exist. These are the areas of a business that need tweaking, although you can't place your finger on exactly what needs changing. These are not the "elephant in the room" kinds of situation, which are more concrete and better defined. I'm talking about perspectives from new hires, employees, and people from other departments or areas of the business that intersect with yours; these individuals can all add valued perspectives. If we asked, sought input or feedback from, or empowered new hires to share what they see, not only would they feel empowered and feel they mattered but people leaders and entire organizations could gain valuable information to mitigate against blind spots. Feeling that you are heard and respected is important and can have a direct impact on a workplace ecosystem.

When workplace needs—such as being heard—are not being met, the fallout can be significant, ranging anywhere from disengagement to burn-out to attrition. In my own career, while I was an employee, I worked with very few leaders who spent the time to create space to get to know me and what I needed. In cases where my needs *were* met, the discretionary and creative energy that was released in my engagement was incredible and moved me to a season of thriving in my career. The challenge for leaders and managers of large teams is especially intense as it takes even more intentional time to invest in each person's unique career journey; therein lies the opportunity for sustained well-being and performance.

The biggest focus in my practice has been to equip leaders and managers with the skills to discover individual and team needs so they can weave them into daily activities. Engaging with your team members and your staff is vital to their success. It leaves them feeling like their efforts are making a difference, that they matter and are truly seen and celebrated. When leaders create the time and space to notice and engage in meaningful conversations, their people are stirred to participate in the task at hand.

What is required is to ask the difficult questions,

"What do you need from me to set you up for success?"
"How can I support you?"

Remember that you don't need to have all the answers: you can discover them together. Knowing your strengths and weaknesses as a leader also helps you hold space for others to work through their own challenges.

And, when we give space to listen, values and needs emerge: that is the art of a great listener and a great leader. Sometimes those needs are unspoken but the basic needs of safety, esteem, belonging, and growth are ubiquitous and cannot be overlooked. The power lies in our ability to understand people's unique needs alongside an appreciation of their natural abilities and contributions to the workplace. In turn, this builds psychological safety and trust in our cultures for our teams to thrive. Remember, when our needs are met (safely expressed, heard, and then actioned), we can be who we are at the most basic levels and perform at our best at the most revolutionary levels.

Leaders are responsible for mattering.

At Your Best

Explore the goals that energize the individuals or teams you are leading and find out what is required of them so they can be at their best; this includes exploring their needs and meeting them where they are at on their growth journey. For example, ask, "How do we get the best of you, and what do you need in order to thrive in your role?"

In listening to what your colleagues' needs are, focus on the whole human and explore the unspoken or hidden needs; consider reflecting on:

- Why are they sharing what they are sharing
- What is being said and what is not being said
- What the heart of the matter is

Radical Conversations

Communication is the real work of leadership

In order to get to a place of deep listening to honour our strengths and needs, we must *lead with curiosity*. By understanding how deeply you want to go or how well you want to get to know a person, consider the types of questions you feel comfortable asking. To create connections, we must go beyond the typical "where-are-you-from-and-what-do-you-do?" small talk. Personally, it feels like my brain goes to sleep during these surface-level exchanges.

According to communication expert, Vanessa Van Edwards, and founder or, Science of People, when we engage in deeper conversations, we start to learn more about people's personalities, values, and goals and learn about what motivates them; we start to unlock dopamine[28]. Dopamine is a known "happiness chemical" so we can start to unlock people's inner worlds and help create the environments for them to feel good and thrive simply by engaging in deeper conversations. This is what we want as people leaders. When connection occurs, and we feel psychologically safe, belonging, trust, and engagement emerge– not only at work but also in life.

These feelings are part of our human relational needs. For example, we can ask,

> "What's been the highlight of your day?"
> "What personal passion project are you working on?"
> "What are you learning at the moment?"
> "What skills would you like to bring to the team?"

This is important in leadership and assists us to be fully able to craft a relationship with consideration for people's personalities and to ensure their behaviours align with individual and team value systems. As people leaders, we can also begin to understand what people believe to be true about themselves. For example, once we have a strong rapport with someone, and psychological safety exists, we can ask,

> "How do you feel most misunderstood?" and
> "What's something most people don't know about you?"

The answers to these questions help us to start to unlock, engage, and connect on a much deeper level. These questions resonated strongly with a particular client who was perceived as an aggressive leader, yet in their heart, they cared deeply and had great ambitions for their career. How, then, could they lean into expressing more of their needs and let their vision fuel their success?

Lead with Inquiry
You won't regret asking questions to get more clarity.

You will regret making a decision based on a story you've created in your own head.

To lead with curiosity, ask open-ended questions, rather than closed-ended questions, such as:
"Do you think…?"
"Have you considered…?"
"Is it okay to…?"
None of the above require a response that draws out further information or demonstrates learning. Closed-ended questions simply give space to literally close the conversation with a simple yes or no answer. A good manager will also discern when it's time to lead with inquiry or give advice, all while assessing the risk, urgency, and impact and discerning if it's a good time for a *Coach-Approach* conversation.

As a leader, in order to extract creativity, engagement, learning, or a change of perspective, predominantly ask "what" or "how" questions. "Tell me more about how you think that meeting went." Asking these open-ended questions is a powerful way to demonstrate curiosity and care and to give space for contribution. Lead with inquiry, ask open-ended questions, and then activate your *Third Ear* for deeper connections. Pick up on the cues of the other person's energy shifts (e.g., can you notice subtle shifts in body language or facial expression?). Challenge assumptions in a caring way, extract learning, and keep moving forward. All of these profound yet simple ways of engaging with others lead to an increase in your relational leadership skills.

A senior manager shared with me once that she felt frustrated because her team ignored the tasks assigned to them. It also seemed there was no accountability; they were unfocused and distracted by other incoming tasks from other departments and busy getting caught up on gossip within the workplace. We explored her previous approaches, such as leading with her positional power: "I'm your manager and have worked here for over a decade, and I know what's best." She then quickly realized that these previous communication habits were sabotaging her efforts to get buy-in from her team. This is called directing and commanding versus building trust and inspiration.

That's where I came in. Through a series of assessments and inquiries, together, we defined the specific actions and reactions that were derailing her leadership effectiveness. Without an objective voice in the conversation with her, she couldn't see what was actually happening.

Through a commitment to becoming the best for her team, she changed her habits by leading with vision, creating the playing field, and asking more open-ended questions about the tasks that needed to be done in relation to the purpose and effectiveness of the team. Even though she admitted it felt like she had to slow down to accelerate the work at hand, she quickly won back her team's respect, one conversation at a time. What she learned is that without understanding how her current communication habits impacted what she wanted most (a healthy, well-bonded team that delivered results), learning new skills was irrelevant.

Language Contributes to Motivation

When someone is told what to do, push-back can show up in many different ways, such as disengagement, sloppy work, or procrastination. This can be particularly activating when we are giving direct feedback. The opportunity when giving feedback is to turn the conversation as quickly as possible into a learning conversation so that contributions or engagement aren't stifled.

So, how can we, as people leaders, use language to invite people into the idea of *wanting to* do something rather than *having to* do it?

Notice the difference between what it feels like when your manager says, with no context regarding a topic that is out of your scope:

"You have to present at this meeting."

Contrast that with how you feel when she says,

"I know it's a bit last minute. Today, there's an opportunity for you to present at a board meeting, and since you are the lead in this area there will be significant agenda item to move this project forward. How would you feel about giving it a go? If you're interested, how can I support you?"

Language changes our relationship to our motivation, our world, and how we show up for ourselves and others. A common question I hear in coaching conversations with leaders is, "How do I motivate this particular individual?" Because motivation is unique to every individual, we must practice asking open-ended questions and listening in order to understand people's deeper motivations and know what they might need to thrive.

Instead of, "you have to," try saying, "would you like to?" or "how would you feel about it?" This same change in energy exists when leaders show up for people with the compassion to better understand their motivations. Instead of telling, try asking open-ended questions to inspire:

"What would it look like when…?"
"How can this decision impact the course of your outcome?"
"What do you need at this point to make a change?"
"What is driving you today?"
"What is stopping you from taking the next step?"
"What support do you need?"

And so on.

When I stepped into my profession as a corporate coach, I had some unlearning to do as my *coaching style* was mostly rooted in sports coaching. In that type of coaching, there was a need to explain and give direct advice on skill and tactical development. Now that I am more assertive in asking questions in my leadership coaching style, I've brought that back into sports coaching which has had a profound impact on the young adults I work with. I now ask players questions such as,

"What worked well?
"What didn't work well in that drill?"
"What did it feel like?"
"Why is it important we have our footwork positioned a certain way?"
"What would happen if this was a game situation?"

I also had a giggle myself when an athlete started giving me an answer, and I replied with, "Oh, tell me more." What I was witnessing was my leadership coaching coming through in the sports coaching. While I recognized there is a certain amount of guidance and mentorship needed when it comes to skill and game tactics, especially with a younger age group, I was creating space for individual and team development by engaging in conversation and reflection rather than simply telling. By asking questions (primarily *what* and *how* questions) and practicing active listening, I was evoking awareness and learning so the answers would come from the players—which is so much better than limiting their experience by constantly telling them what to do.

Part of the leadership equation is to continuously pay attention to relational communication skills. You can measure this by the engagement of your people: are they coming to you with ideas and contributions? Are you asking what their needs are and staying curious about what is driving their productivity and what is stopping them? By holding this perspective of what the current reality is versus where you want to go, you are able to discern at what point they need more support, and at which point you can let them do the good work. What's important here is that we stay in the learning zone—both personally and professionally—in our leadership practice.

Reflect to Grow

The Coach-Approach

Review the Levels of Listening and identify when you can hold space for others and when you cannot. What is required so you can be more present as you engage your team members?

Next time you're in a one-on-one meeting or checking in with a colleague, try asking a *what* or *how* question to evoke a deeper connection.

Listen more, speak less.

CHAPTER 12

Learning Zone

A goal of leadership is to keep people in the learning zone.

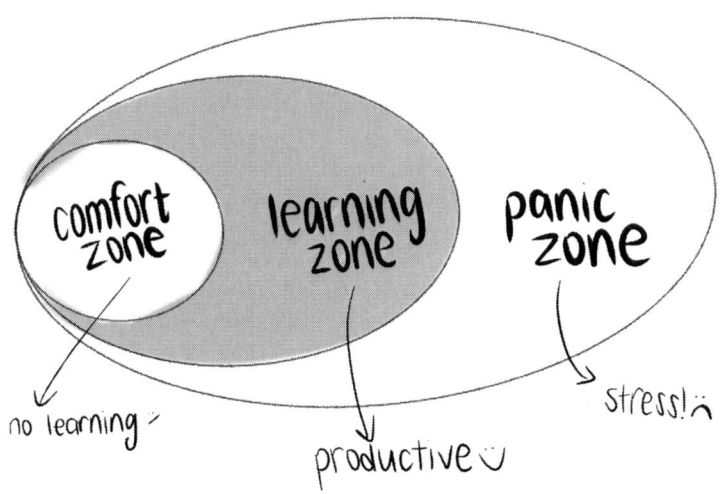

Learning Zone

Capturing learning moments is a sure way to create psychologically safe work environments because it keeps an active, reflective practice embedded in a culture of performance[29]. If we are not learning, we are not growing. The learning zone is defined in many ways. It's a place where you're challenged and engaged rather than bored. It is a space when you are encouraged and inspired rather than fearful of making mistakes. You may feel a healthy level of stress, but you can enjoy it. The learning zone is the sweet spot of performance nestled between the comfort zone and the panic zone. If we are in the comfort zone or panic zone, there is no learning. The learning zone is the productive or performance zone.

The key here is to induce the right amount of challenge stress, meaning that the pressure is high but not so high that people disengage. Every company, team, and person will have their own level of challenge or performance stress that they can sustain during different times which is why creating space for learning moments in the culture of high performance is paramount. When people are not stretched outside of what they already know, their energy will plateau, or, alternatively, if they are overstretched, there may be significant costs to well-being and performance.

I led a workshop focusing on company culture and how to help team members stay in their learning zones several years ago for a group of respected managers. I was thrilled that the managers found new ways to intentionally reflect on and capture moments of learning: after a successful or challenging client engagement, for example, or at the start of a meeting, or the end of a consulting project. As a result, participants knew when to accelerate and raise the performance challenge by setting bigger goals, or when it was necessary to pause and work through the current realities of the challenges at hand. When capturing the learning moments of new hires, for example, it's important to know how much more to add to their plate. We all learn at different speeds, so to keep up with change, we must take a moment to pause, ask, listen, reflect and then build on the takeaways.

Staying in the learning zone means we can give space to failures or setbacks and learn from mistakes. Sure, learning can happen through many modalities like reading or reflecting; however, true learning happens through experience and even more so when we experience failure in our leadership practice. Learning makes performance fun and also allows us to build on what is working well. If we can name it, then we can claim it and aim it towards future tasks. Leadership creates an environment of psychologically safe workplaces. If there's too much change and consistent turbulence (whether the company is growing fast or laying off a lot of employees); I've seen intentional pauses to reflect and the habit of staying in the learning zone are what sustain a team most. What is helpful when managing people through change is to stay in the learning.

Harvard psychologist Amy Edmondson, speaks about the value of staying in the learning zone (or performance zone) and how it relates to creating and sustaining safety in the workplace[30]. If I feel, "it's okay for me to admit a mistake" or bring forth a challenge, then I have perceived emotional and psychological safety, that even though I made a mistake, I can learn from the experience. This requires leadership to be open and inviting to role modeling their own fallibility and intentionally capturing learning moments.

Psychological safety is a basic human need. To perform, to be, to exist, and to thrive, we must feel safe so we can also activate the creative parts of our brains. When we do not feel safe, we are stuck in fight-or-flight mode. Better to move past the limbic system of the brain to the neocortex and unleash the potential of creativity and thought and activate our dreams. Forethought or imagination lives in the conscious part of the brain, but when our amygdala is "hijacked," we cannot move towards it.

Edmondson gives the example that when hospital teams feel safe to admit errors, overall, they perform better. This is an indication of the openness of the climate of the work environment and leadership sets the tone for this.

Equally important is that when safety and learning habits are at the forefront of high-performance workplace cultures, that does not mean we neglect accountability. In fact, accountability and action are part of the formula for high-performance teams. Holding space for performance lies in the narrative of how we capture learnings and hold people accountable for their actions. It's a dance between being supportive and raising the challenge while letting up on the breaks of perfection. *Your leadership practice is not a pursuit of perfection but a journey of attention.*

>*Excellence* is enduring
>Perfection is fleeting
>
>*Excellence* is risk
>Perfection is fear
>
>*Excellence* is striving
>Perfection is demanding
>
>*Excellence* is freeing
>Perfection is stifling
>
>*Excellence* is confidence
>Perfection is doubt
>
>*Excellence* is a journey
>Perfection is a destination

Junior World Cup

Shifting the narrative to sports for a moment, I'd like to share a leadership challenge my colleagues and I endured at the Junior Women's Field Hockey World Cup in Santiago, Chile in 2023.

At the competition, we were faced with a daunting task. Ranked 18th in the world, we had brought our under 21 Canadian field hockey team to play at the Junior World Cup, the highest competition in the world for this age group. As a nation, technically and tactically, we were evidently behind due to a variety of factors such as the accessibility of the sport in Canada. Regardless of our challenges, we brought together seventeen athletes from all over North America to compete and proudly represent our country.

Every defeat taught us more about our game. Yes, we learned more about tactics and technical skills but even more importantly, we realized we could focus on our mindsets, attitudes, and process goals.

As coaches, our goal was to keep the athletes in the learning zone and to keep morale high regardless of the score line. By the end of the tournament, the athletes shared how not only how they had grown as players but also as people–learning to manage the demands of high-performance environments, being supportive teammates, balancing academics with sport, reflecting on their growth, and showing up repeatedly. So, how did we accomplish this shift in perspective?

At the Junior World Cup, we focused on:

- Celebrating incremental growth and measuring process goals (how many attacking opportunities we could create per half) versus outcome goals (winning or losing)
- Reviewing the health of the team culture and being reminded of our own playing field (who we are, why we exist, and how we behave). What could we control within the context of the high-performance environment?
- Actively managing recovery modalities—physical, mental, and emotional
- Holding space for reflections and learning, and all the emotions that the sport has to offer
- Most importantly, keeping the joy!

Sport and performance exist to expand all aspects of our humanness, and this experience did just that—not only for the athletes, but also for the coaches. *We needed to capture the learning moments to keep our spirits high and embrace our losses.* The goal was to extract learnings while honouring the athletes' well-being and performance challenges, and we did just that.

Safety Builds Trust

The by-product of staying in the learning zone is that people want to contribute, and you are providing space for people to feel challenged yet cared for, to be at their best, with their full selves, mistakes included. This is why social and emotional safety builds trust. Trust is the foundation of a thriving relationship. It is critical to understand that it involves how someone feels. When you experience good leadership, you feel safe and can be more creative, leveraging the executive function of the brain.

Team culture is also built on a foundation of trust (as is suggested in Patrick Lencioni's book, The Five Dysfunctions of a Team[31]). As we build teams or groups of people who are working together towards a common goal and purpose, we need to begin with a complex understanding of trust. Honest, open discussions about trust set the stage for deeper, more productive conversations about team performance and, importantly, create stronger connections.

Employees in high-trust organizations are more productive, have more energy at work, collaborate better with their colleagues, and stay with their employers longer than those working at low-trust companies[32]. They also suffer less chronic stress and are happier with their lives, and these factors fuel stronger performance. But how do you do that effectively?

As leaders, if our challenge is to move people from A to B, we need trust. If people don't trust us, they won't follow us. So, how do we create trust? After connecting to your intention to build a culture of trust, consider the following behaviours that contribute greatly to high-trust environments. In reading through, note where you want to focus your trust-building skills as a leader.

1. **Be consistent in how you show up**
   In building a culture of trust, consistency is probably the most important energy you can contribute to your ecosystem. Day in and day out, how are you showing up? Are you in tune with your own nervous system and energy before showing up with chaos in your head and heart or with clarity of the task at hand? *People respond to the way a leader shows up.* A client once shared that they had a documented spreadsheet of how to respond, behave, and act, depending on the mood of how their manager showed up on any given day! Imagine how much discretionary energy went into managing their manager's mood instead of the work that needed to get done. So, first, master your mood.

2. **Invest in getting to know your people**
   The surest and quickest way to get to know your people is to see people for who they are, identify their strengths and needs (as discussed in Chapter 11) and set the expectations for connection. Unfortunately, this is not a one-time activity; it requires an intentional, deliberate, ongoing practice. It requires scheduling weekly one-on-one meetings with them, creating space for career development conversations, and reminding people why you are doing what you are doing. The *Coach-Approach* skills are relevant here as you express interest in and concern for team members' success and personal well-being. Talk less, listen more.

3. **Recognition matters**

    Neuroscience shows that recognition has the largest effect on trust when it occurs immediately after a goal has been met, when it comes from peers, and when it's tangible, unexpected, personal, and public[33]. This may of course change depending on the individual but overall, the experiences of recognition, being seen, and being valued are human needs and its crucial leaders practise them. Leaders I work with often agree they need to be better at this, mostly because it takes a commitment of time and energy to hold space for these types of moments. I've also seen leaders who praise abundantly but the praise is not coming from a genuine place, or they are so vague that the person receiving it cannot authentically accept the recognition. There is an art and a science to this simple yet complex need to recognize excellence. Start by recognizing the individual and team strengths in action.

4. **Stretch your comfort zone**

    When your people trust you, meaning you will catch them if they fall, you can take them to the edges of their performance. Moving out of a comfort zone often evokes self-doubt and insecurities, yet it is also how we grow, learn, and develop. The last thing we want is when individuals feel bored, stifling their engagement and creativity. Knowing a person feels psychologically and emotionally safe to fail and they trust you won't hold it against them is a sure way to stretch the comfort zone. What is required here is that you have ensured (as best as you can) that you have instilled beliefs in them and given them the best conditions to meet a new edge.

5. **Hold people capable and accountable**
Keeping people in the performance and learning zone ensures you hold people accountable for their tasks at hand, and this builds trust. Recently, a client shared with me that the same tasks were consistently not being done every two weeks with different excuses emerging in team meetings. It became clear through our conversations that this leader was too shy to name the lack of accountability rather than to call it out and be curious about the actions in the way of the team's ability to move forward. For example, important information was actually missing, which prevented his team members from completing the tasks but they didn't feel safe enough to bring this forward. As a leader, even though you want to adopt the belief that everyone is capable of completing the work, it's also part of your role to ensure the *work gets done.* When we keep the work at the centre of the conversation, it gives us permission to lean in and hold people accountable.

6. **Extend autonomy**
This is particularly relevant in the strengths conversation. When we recognize we all have our own way of doing something, we can give space for the "how." At the same time, leaders must show team members why a task is important, and they must articulate the overall vision or performance goal. Autonomy also promotes innovation because different people have different approaches to creative work, having difficult conversations, and so forth. Most clients I work with do not like to be micromanaged, so the task clearly becomes to lead with expectation setting so each person can get the work done the best way they know.

7. **Be Transparent**

    Ongoing communication is key: A 2015 study of 2,500,000 manager-led teams in 195 countries found that workforce engagement improved when supervisors had some form of daily communication with their direct reports[34]. Yes, this is particularly valuable and necessary when change is on the horizon. Being transparent about the changes going on in the workplace is a key practice in sharing information when the time is right. Beyond information sharing, transparency about your feelings, strengths, and weaknesses is a sure way to build trust. Transparency builds trust.

8. **Yes, be vulnerable**

    Asking for help is effective because it taps into the natural human impulse to cooperate with others. If only this were easier done than said. Asking for help or saying, "I don't know," is a key attribute for building trust as leaders. There might be a part of you that you need to put aside so you can show more vulnerability in your leadership practice. We cannot grow in our trust practice unless we are willing to be vulnerable. Through role modelling vulnerability, we deepen our connections, develop compassion, and move towards collective growth and learning. While people are impressed by your strengths, they connect more with you on a human level through your weaknesses.

Reflect to Grow

Safety Builds Trust
Rate the leadership qualities in your efforts to build trust from 1 (poor) to 5 (excellent). Which trust-building characteristics can you be more intentional with? What is one action you can take to move the dial?

- ☐ Consistent in how I show up
- ☐ Investing in getting to know my people
- ☐ Recognition, acknowledging, celebrating
- ☐ Holding people capable and accountable
- ☐ Extending trust and autonomy
- ☐ Stay in the learning zone
- ☐ Being transparent
- ☐ Being vulnerable
- ☐ Other:

CHAPTER 13

Thriving Teams

Leadership is about enabling others to thrive

Since most of our working world involves working with people, within teams, or as a group of people coming together to work towards a common goal, knowing how to effectively collaborate is necessary. The word collaboration itself translates as "co-labour." Working collaboratively has the potential to ignite joy and move people towards thriving. It feels good to accomplish tasks together. It feels good to win. It feels good when you have a meaningful connection. It feels good when you can celebrate together. So, how do we pull all these pieces together, from setting up the playing field to living out values, for talents to shine, and for us to be well at the end of the day?

Team Culture in Sport

The stakes are perpetually high at the championship events in any high-performance sporting arena —be it tennis, hockey, football, rugby or another sporting discipline. Nerves and skills are pushed to the limit. When competing in a team sport, we must remember our contributions are only as productive as the total output. This was showcased in the summer of 2022 when two of the top field hockey nations came together at the World Cup final in Valencia, Spain. The great Argentina versus the Netherlands. Argentina was fuelled by immense talent that saw their individual players single-handedly leave behind players from other nations repeatedly throughout the tournament. Their skill made it look as though they were merely practising, dancing around their opponents without much disruption. Yet, in the final game, it was clear they were not able to win on individual talent alone.

The Dutch were flawless in their team performance. Passes were crisp and on point; there was no individual hero; this was a collective workforce. Up and down the 100-yard field, they flew until the final whistle. Each moment was captivating to watch: how did the players know where the others would be as they sent 30- and 40-yard passes into open spaces? On defence, they moved as a pack; every player knew their role in keeping the defence tight and did not allow the skillful, but solo, Argentinian players to shatter their efforts. The team from the Netherlands took the crown in a brilliant illustration of moving together like a well-oiled machine. The team knew who they were and why they were playing that game. Talent was in action; the game plan had been activated and the performance followed with radiant confidence.

What led to this world-class performance? What allowed flow to happen in such a high-stakes environment? We saw not only a brilliant performance and outcome but also a culture, a system, and the collective energy of people which had been built over time through discipline, deep study, and a commitment to the best of each person—*that's* what fueled the success of the team from the Netherlands.

What if we shifted away from sports and looked at the industry of broadcasting live sporting events? There is no rehearsal when there's a live event. So, how do broadcasting teams know who does what and by when? These teams execute with such precision and vision in a context that provides no room for noise and disengagement. Imagine you're televising the Wimbledon Tennis Final Championship. You have people on the court, in the studio, on social media and in the editing suite. All players are on deck. The challenge is met with great execution. Each person knows their role, what value they add, why they are there, and what success looks like.

When the goal is clear (and the people are in the safe, enabling conditions where they are seen, heard and feel they belong), performance follows. When the goal is clear, accountability and feedback are offered in pursuit of that goal. It's difficult to hold people accountable or provide recognition or constructive feedback about performance when there are no agreed *Ways of Working* and goals are not aligned.

Now, in sports, we see performance outcomes through a measure of goals scored/lost, points lost or accumulated, and so forth. But what about the intangible development and value of character that transpires through sports? The same is true in the workplace. As leaders, part of the pursuit of productivity requires you to pay attention to the development of people's character, their personal and professional development, and your team's overall well-being. This is where team performance and well-being intersect so workplace teams thrive.

Workplace Performance and Well-being

When teams and their members are distracted, disengaged, unrecognized or unaligned around a common playing field, the potential of their performance and well-being is compromised. In cases where both well-being and performance are low, there is a state of being **unrealized**—where conflict may be high, and trust is low. Sure, an individual may take the initiative to succeed or drive their contribution on their own but inevitably they will sacrifice their well-being in pursuit of success. This is the instance where performance is high, well-being is low, and we are **siloed**. Burn-out is a common theme here when independent, perfectionist behaviour kicks in. I have also worked with teams who are highly **connected** and have a strong sense of their needs being met, yet still their performance is low, with no accountability for their results.

The dance between participating in a high-performance team environment is met at the intersection of well-being and performance.

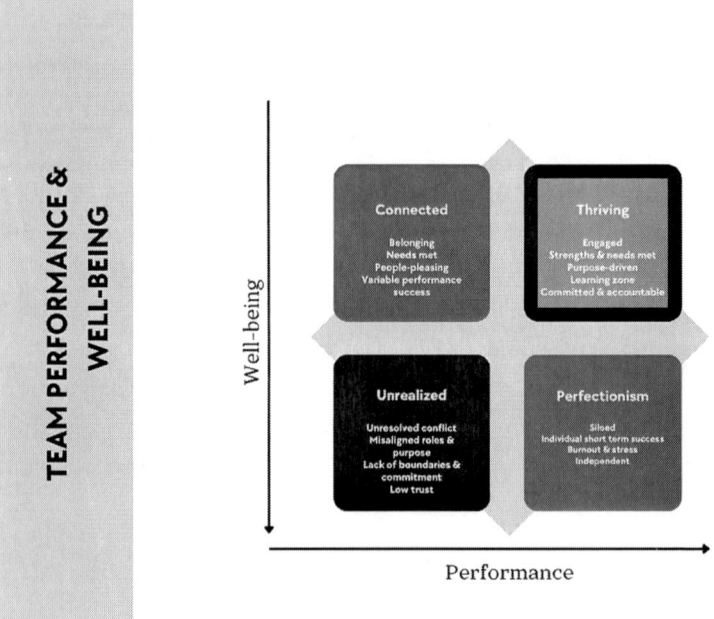

Team Performance and Wellbeing

In this sweet spot of **thriving**, when well-being and performance are both high, we have the Playing Field set up. We have leadership and peers focusing on recognizing and working with strengths and meeting each other's needs. There is alignment on purpose and direction, with mutual accountability and commitment to do good work together. When we have a thriving team, the leader of the team can shift their energy to the strategic priorities of the work at hand, continue to cast vision, keep people in the learning zone, and practising the *Coach-Approach* their team requires.

I have worked with numerous team leaders who enter this zone and find joy and freedom within the fluidity of the frameworks. We can work with frameworks but must always be aware that human performance and behaviour are complex and will continue to evolve and shift and change. Performance challenges also change as team members move through personal and professional development phases.

Moving to Thriving Teams

Ensuring all members of your team are on the same playing field will elicit a thriving culture. Remember, the *Playing Field*—or the act of holding space for performance—is a metaphor for the conditions necessary for the success and well-being of a team or a group of people. It's a framework that allows them to engage with others so everyone can feel mentally and emotionally safe to participate, grow, learn, and innovate. The outcome is incremental growth which allows us to stay in the learning zone of performance.

1. **Know yourself.** Regardless of the talent or the team, success stems from knowing who you are as a leader and understanding how that relates to your role in creating high-performance cultures. I have yet to find a leader who has it all—exceptional strategic, relationship, influencing, and execution skills. Learn how to leverage your unique leadership qualities to benefit your team.
2. **Know your team's individual and group strengths and needs** so you can set each other up for success. This helps ensure the right people are in the right roles where their interests are met and aligned with the needs of the business. Spend time on "job crafting" (more on this in Part 3).

3. **Know the health of your team** either through company engagement surveys or team culture assessments that measure the levels of trust, effectiveness, commitment, and ability to have healthy conflict. Know where you are today and where you're heading. Get clear on your *Ways of Working* so your values can guide your behaviour. These sessions are important for aligning behaviours with your values, fostering cohesion, building psychological safety, and ensuring mutual accountability.
4. **Apply the Coach-Approach** to your daily informal and formal interactions in the workplace, particularly in your regular individual and team meetings. Demonstrate and affirm that you believe in your people so they feel like you're setting them up for success and consider them capable.
5. **Establish intentional engagement and planning with your people.** Include culture and people development as a business strategy in your annual strategic plans and goals. Dedicate time to team-building, team-coaching, and conversations dedicated to individuals' performance and careers. Don't let your people strategy fall to the bottom of your to-do list. Your people are your business.
6. **Facilitation is an art and a science**. Group, team, or individual discussions blossom with skilled and rotated facilitation. Organizations also benefit from external facilitators who are unbiased, unattached, non-judgmental, and have no positional power. A perceived threat of power can significantly impact the quality of conversation.

At the heart of inspired leadership lies the quality of our connection to ourselves and the people we engage with. People need to know you are fully invested in them as human beings to thrive in their work lives and although practicing relational leadership qualities takes intentional effort it is required to make teams work. It takes courage and vulnerability to create synergies in the world of work and bring out the best in each person.

Reflect to Grow

Thriving Teams
Assess the health of your team culture through assessments (e.g., Team Culture BluePrint™), customized culture surveys and/or individual and focus group conversations. What does your team need to be well, to perform well?

PART 3
To US

THRIVING ECOSYSTEMS

PART 3: INTRODUCTION

Now that you've covered the fundamentals of agency (Part 1) and relational leadership skills (Part 2), this final section gets to the heart of practicing leadership and why it matters. Part 3 explores the impact that leadership practices have on *us* as a collective. We look at how our leadership impacts our well-being and why it is necessary to continuously practice leadership as part of an everyday action for sustained performance.

Leadership is not just for the person next to you; it's also within and applicable to the different ecosystems to which you belong. *Leadership is a practice we all participate in.* While our personal leadership work is important for our individual lives, its importance is amplified when we lead and engage with others in the workplace, at home, or in our communities.

During my time on the African continent, I learned a beautiful word, *Ubuntu*, which means "I am because you are." It's a concept that expresses the fact that we are all in this together. When individuals, teams, organizations and communities adopt an attitude and practice of *Ubuntu*, abundant compassionate outcomes will follow because it means we have each other; I can't be fully me without you. We need each other; my humanity is tied to yours. I often saw *Ubuntu* in practice during my lived experiences in South-Eastern Africa. These are the attitudes and behaviours that we can learn, unlearn, and relearn as we move through our leadership growth journeys. What follows in this part of the book are leadership stories that have shaped much of my life's work and perspectives on how leadership directly impacts the ecosystems in which we all exist.

Part 3 explores why your impact matters in an ecosystem and how well-being must be at the forefront. Applying your personal mastery to how you manage positions of power and lead people through change is also essential to your leadership practice. It's well to remember that emotional intelligence is also required if we want to understand our mindset and attitudes and effectively lead others and contribute to society through our leadership.

CHAPTER 14

Your Impact Matters

Leadership is defined by the difference you make.

The call for the 21st century is for responsible leadership.

As leaders, we need to lead people from a place of knowing who we are, and the values that drive our behaviours, and what responsibility we carry. Responsible leadership is about being human-centred, which requires us to know all the parts of ourselves and to be curious about the people around us and how we can contribute to the most complex challenges of our times. It's up to each person to know their authentic leadership and define what responsible leadership means to them. Some ideas on the topic of responsible leadership include:

Responsible leadership is about personal leadership.

Responsible leadership is about the triple bottom line: people, planet, and profit.

Responsible leadership is about making a positive impact.

To lead responsibly means to lead sustainably.

Leadership shapes culture whether or not you are doing so intentionally. Culture impacts performance and well-being. When we practice leadership beyond ourselves, we advance purpose-driven, human-centred behaviour which contributes to the way we work and play, and to the greater good of the world. You might wonder what your spheres of influence are, exactly. While we can think of spheres of influence on many levels, let's start with the areas closest to you: your immediate relationships and the people you surround yourself and engage with. Our leadership takes shape in these micro-engagements. Your daily impact matters in the workplace, on a family level, and in your communities.

We could endlessly define what responsible leadership looks like and this is a unique opportunity to examine what it means to you. By the end of Part 3, I hope you can define this in tangible ways for yourself.

The following story of a lived experience in rural Southern Africa catalyzed my aspirations to work in leadership development. While I had been drawn to the fields of sociology and psychology during my academic pursuits, this later experience brought together the idea of empowering others while recognizing how culture impacts our societies. Since culture is about people's collective thinking, working with individuals at the grassroots levels made sense at the time, or so I thought.

At this moment in time, I was working with Swaziland Action Group Against Abuse (SWAGGA), a non-governmental organization that exists to end gender-based violence.

> **Trigger Warning:**
>
> **Please note there are some details about sexual violence in the following story that may impact readers.**

SWAGAA Experience

It was a day when my empathy caught up with me the minute I got home to my apartment and sat down to indulge in a meal with my roommate. Most days, I am a processor. It takes me minutes, days, and even weeks to crystalize my thoughts, process my experiences, and to be able to articulate how I am feeling. This day however was different because I cried the moment I got home safely.

During my first years of supporting international development programs that fought against gender-based violence against women in Eswatini, it was common for me to take the local bus—or "kombi"—to and from work. Oftentimes, I would just pray that I got to and from where I needed to go alive. I was often the lone white girl tightly sandwiched in the kombi between people, children, and even wildlife. Chickens, yes, there were chickens near me, often. I would treat the experience like it was normal most of the time as the kombi drove at unbearable speeds, starting and stopping suddenly enough that the doorman would regularly fly off the side of the kombi before or after he hustled passengers in to join the ride.

Working in the field of international development was mostly uplifting, inspiring and supportive: I was contributing to our programs' progress. This particular day started out the same as every other day. But something shifted inside me. The kombi arrived at the main stop in Manzini town centre and I exited. I passed through the hustle and bustle of the dynamic, beautifully bright roadside markets, local produce stands, and heckling from men. I got to the building where the SWAGAA office, a haven for abused women, was housed. This is an important organization in the nation, which has a high rate of gender-based violence against women. The statistics report that one in three women under the age of sixteen is raped. While I recognize that this is an international travesty, the infrastructure and legal support was not yet put in place to protect those abused. The program I was contributing to was part of an intervention to empower mentors and set up empowerment clubs for girls in schools. The goal was to build confidence in and educate young women across the country to stand up for themselves and say "no," to affirm their human rights and assist them in believing in their dreams and aspirations. Back then, in 2013, the legislature still had not yet passed a law-making rape illegal. Women were not protected, even by law. The funding partners and local partners of the SWAGAA had set up almost 100 of these girls' empowerment clubs.

On the day in question, I was set to join my local counterparts at a school in an extremely rural area, a school far away from any town or village, known as an "inkundla." Travelling along red-soiled gravel roads had become normal to me at this time, and having driven a company's car out on numerous site visits I had become adept at dodging the worst of the potholes that were spaced every few meters along the road. When we got to the school, the principal greeted us with a warm "Sawubona," which is a beautiful word in Zulu that is both a greeting and an expression of "I see you." I responded with a big "Yebo" (meaning, "Yes, I receive that you see me, and I see you as well.")

We decided how we were going to engage the young women who were in early high school and between about fourteen and sixteen years of age. We had prepared questions and exercises for the girls to reflect on, and after some dialogue, we sat in small groups. I sat in a group that included four young women. It was quiet, the usual silence when you meet a stranger and are asked to share your thoughts in a foreign language. I remember sitting there, focused on being present and listening. I must have listened for more than an hour to the stories. Unimaginable stories. Stories of rape. Stories of bribery. Stories of pain and suffering. Stories that girls in this village lived with daily. They openly gifted me with their trust. It was powerful, with many moments when girls told their stories for the first time. These stories put life into perspective: *"To come to school, I must perform with my uncle so that he will pay for my school fees."*

There were stories about abuse, rape, and the reality of their lived experiences. I think this is the moment when I realized the power of holding space, a key coaching skill that allows the coach to be in the moment and listen to what the client is not saying. In this case, underneath the stories the girls shared was fear; they were not safe unless they were here at school, in this space. Some girls were ashamed. Some shared about early pregnancies and being banned from school. Some girls were angry. Their emotions fluttered in every direction. I had no answers, but I knew that this exercise, the questions I asked, and the space I held was the start of what needed to be seen, to be heard.

I share this experience of the day in the field at this school with those young women because, at this moment, I realized our work for a better world is much bigger than funding to provide young women (and men) with the skills to build their confidence. In fact, our work for change has got to go from the top down. Let's suppose we work on the mindset and confidence of young women to go home and say "no" when there are no laws to protect them. This was true at the time, and since then protective laws have been passed due to the persevering work of SWAGAA and its stakeholders.

What happens then? *And how can we shift the hearts and minds of people from the top down?*

What role does leadership play in cultures to shift paradigms that bring out the best in people? Why is the government making exorbitant school fees mandatory so family members abuse the very young who need the education? We need to bring many stakeholders into the complexities of the above issue.

> This experience filled my heart with many questions. What *does it mean to lead a safe home? What does it mean to lead a school where children are safe? What role does*

leadership—formal or informal—play in the impact of people's well-being? What does responsible leadership truly mean at all levels of society?

While my experience in Eswatini was related to basic human rights—the need for safety to attend school, to have access to basic education, to be nourished, and to feel safe at home—it was the beginning of the call for my work as a leadership consultant and coach. We need to accelerate change, both at home and work, and tap into our truest selves so we can lead our lives for the greater good of humanity. And invite people to enthusiastically bring their human skills to work, knowing they are not quietly brutalized on their home front. If not us, then who? If not now, then when?

"If you think you're too small to have an impact, try going to bed with a mosquito."

- Anonymous

Change can't happen only at the bottom through empowering young children. Culture change requires the work of adults who understand their agency. True change needs to come both from the top down and bottom up, but it's not just that, either; change is all around us in our ecosystems. The holistic facets of our leadership practice have an immense impact on all of *us*.

While this is one example of all the stories of pain and injustice in our world today, how does our leadership practice stay in pursuit of the greater good? And whose responsibility is it to ensure this happens?

A responsible leader:

- builds empowerment by believing in others' abilities and encouraging their strengths
- is courageous and models integrity, humility, and vulnerability and,
- catalyzes change by taking actions to positively contribute to their ecosystem.

And responsible leadership is for all of us.

Reflect to Grow

Your Impact
What positive contribution do you want to make to the lives of others? In what ecosystems can you create more awareness of the effects of leadership decisions?

Where might your intentions not be aligned with the desired impact you want to have? How will you know?

CHAPTER 15

Leadership and Power

Leadership asks us to exercise both formal and informal power

The topic of power is important to all humans; it plays a significant role in our leadership practice, and how we lead impacts our peers, families, teams, communities, and the next generation. As we've explored honouring our journey of leading ourselves in Part 1 and then leaning into the skills of leading others in Part 2, we now want to consider how the fruits of our leadership practice impact those around us. Before we do, we must attune to the power we carry within us.

What do a sports coach, a teacher, a manager, a CEO, a parent, and a person who has positional power have in common? They all have authority and the potential to impact many people deeply—for better or worse. Regardless of the role you find yourself in and the positional power of that role, you need to be aware of it and use it wisely. Even if you don't carry a role of authority (by explicit title), you carry within you a great deal of personal power, as discussed in Part 1. This power stems from all your lived experiences, strengths, knowledge, and inner wisdom. We all have spheres of influence and hold different forms of power, so the question is, *how do you want to use your personal or positional power to positively impact the people around you?*

What Gets in the Way?
Regardless of how we see power show up in our leadership practice, it matters. There are common temptations or needs humans naturally have that may also disrupt your practice of exerting meaningful heart-based leadership in the communities to which you contribute. We often see the misuse of power in our lives when someone's ego gets in the way. The unchecked "ego self" potentially has unhealthy needs that, when not unveiled and managed, can damage trust in our relationships and negatively affect our collaboration with others. We must understand we all have egos and human needs; they are normal. The question becomes, to what degree are our needs healthy or to what degree do they interfere with the work at hand?

The intention of looking at our needs as they relate to leadership and power is that when we have authority in a role we carry a great responsibility to practice impactful leadership that supports and enables others, not causing harm or diminishing their potential.

As you reflect on the needs listed below, evaluate if they feel healthy or exaggerated in your current role or position of power:

Need for Control, Influence
I've seen leaders exercise a strong degree of control and they have had a hard time giving the work back to people with the autonomy required for the work to get done. This can stem from many places; for example, people who grew up in a chaotic environment often want to create order to feel safe. However, creating structure and using control, power, or influence to exert this need in the workplace can damage morale. In this instance, trust can be compromised, and people's development and creativity can be stifled. Nobody likes to be micromanaged.

Need for Significance, Recognition

Humility is a practice of giving credit where credit is due and is the antidote to excessively seeking recognition. When out of control, leaders can mislead people with answers or certainty they don't have, or take credit for the work of others to boost their individual significance. When the need for significance predominates, it can prevent an individual from moving towards the greater purpose of doing meaningful work beyond the self. This need also flares its head in a "ladder" type organization where, at any cost, people will put their own need for a title promotion, a salary increase, or other means of perceived significance, ahead of recognizing what the team or organization needs from them. The danger here is a fleeting sense of when "enough" becomes enough.

Need for Belonging, Intimacy

Another area leaders must tend to is the need for belonging, validation, or intimacy—the need to be liked and accepted by everyone. While these are all important factors in the workplace, they can become unhealthy or "unchecked," inhibiting performance or crossing boundaries of professionalism and workplace safety. I have heard many personal stories of people using their positional authority to meet their intimacy needs. This can also show up in the workplace when an individual stays silent and puts the need to belong over their ambitions or their willingness to contribute a differing opinion. The exaggerated need for belonging can stem from a childhood of "not fitting in" or other early experiences in family or personal life. Being aware that you are trying to befriend and be liked by everyone can hinder your performance and stifle your leadership potential.

Managing Needs

Needs drive human behaviour and they impact our leadership practice. When needs go unchecked and become unhealthy in the workplace, they are particularly amplified for those in a position of power. Thus, the reflection here is to take care of your whole self and seek counsel to support your blind spots or those parts of your leadership practice you might not yet be conscious of.

Take care of your needs, so they don't become distractions to the work at hand. When you recognize a certain need is not healthy, you can remind yourself of who you are in your truest, wisest "self," how you want to show up, and stay anchored in your values, purpose, and vision. This is a continuous practice which requires a high degree of vulnerability and commitment to being accountable and living with integrity.

Only you, as the leader, can give space to reflect on any unhealthy needs you may have and how they may impact your leadership and the work you are committed to doing. Addressing unconscious unhealthy needs reveals patterns and fears, as well as hopes, dreams, and desires.

Imagine if we could lean into the art and science of practicing responsible leadership so our power exists to enable others, rather than to constrain them.

Leadership in the 21st century is about creating the ecosystem for your family, team, organization, or nation to find the spaces to grow and develop based on individual aspirations and dreams. It's about "doing good" beyond the self. The world depends on it. Our planet depends on it. Our quality of life depends on it.

So, when you think of power consider both how you're practicing your personal power and how you might impact the world even without a formal title. At the same time, recognize when you're in a place of a positional power and how your behaviours impact others. The opportunity is to choose how you want to positively impact your own life and those you lead - be it at home, work, or in sport.

Reflections on Power:

- Transformational leaders *empower others* rather than use power to get what they want.
- When we honour our personal power, we don't shy away from roles of positional power.
- The power we give to those who hold a title can limit or enhance the use of our personal power.
- When you lean into your power, you get to amplify your vision, values, and purpose.
- Leadership power creates spaces for voices to be included and for differences to be celebrated.
- The power of privilege can support people with less privilege.
- Power is not scary or harmful, yet acknowledging your power and the impact you want to have is a way to actively participate in building a better world.

Reflect to Grow

Your Personal Board of Directors

We can't do this work of leadership alone. Who are your mentors or your confidants in your personal and professional spaces that can offer you wise counsel? Think of this as having your own personal board of directors: who is lifting you higher and keeping you accountable to your development as a leader? What advice would they give you about managing your needs and catalyzing your personal power for positive change?

CHAPTER 16

Change, Transitions, and Growth

Leadership is in the business of managing change and transitions

As leaders, we are in the business of making transitions and managing change—in ourselves and in those we lead. Life is complex, people are complex, and change is inevitable. How do we show love and compassion while managing transitions and complexities so people's hearts and minds remain at the forefront of performance?

We've all gone through the process of change in one form or another but what happens when we seek to change—or even when it is imposed upon us? What factors influence change, and what does it feel and look like?

A change might be big or small, yet an inevitable process occurs—both internally and externally. *Change happens externally and moving through the emotional and psychological transition happens internally.* We can't see the emotional and mental transition process as much as we can see the physical change (such as moving to a new city, starting a new relationship, changing jobs, starting or ending a habit, etc.). As humans, we are constantly making decisions—again, some are big and some are small. If we can learn to recognize we are going through a process of change we can name the feelings and circumstances, accept them, and then surround ourselves with the support we need to move through the change. The process becomes fluid and we can ride the waves intentionally. This process of naming the change and being transparent about it is especially important when mobilizing people during turbulent times.

Sometimes, change is sprung upon us. Sometimes, we don't have the luxury of contemplating all the steps in the process. But it's important to give space (and grace) to the external change and catch up with the internal transition by managing our emotions. Recall the story I shared of the director who had to lay off more than fifty team members and the complexities that were going on both inside himself and within the department? Everyone has a different tolerance for change. Abrupt change can feel difficult, and we don't always have the luxury of incremental growth towards change. The good news is that we can equip ourselves for the process of it.

When there is a choice involved in the change, and it includes multiple people or stakeholders, and we can discuss the change to gather perspectives and information, people are more likely to contribute and co-create the new vision. This work requires transformational leadership—empowering people along the way instead of telling them what to do.

It's also important to focus on the emotions of change, and part of that process involves letting go—letting go of loss, grief, and a future direction which is no longer true. As I've learned in life, grief is a way for love to find a new home. Feel the emotions of grief, loss, and change, and know that as you gently examine this process, a new normal will emerge, and there's something waiting for you on the other side. I celebrate organizational leaders who create space for grief – be it in experiencing loss when a leader leaves, in a personal capacity, or simply in recognizing when the organization is moving through change. The feeling of being stuck arises when one part of us wishes to experience a certain known state while another part of us is resisting the experience in front of us. Honour what is in front of you, hold space for the unknown and move through the experience expecting the unexpected.

Ultimately, moving through change while managing the transition and making space for growth requires a great deal of courage. And guess what? We can learn and grow together.

Moving Away From and Moving Towards

When considering change, we are motivated to move away from something or towards something. For example, we either want to move away from spending money on unhealthy habits or we want to create a healthy lifestyle that energizes us. We either want to stay connected to our values or live out of misalignment. We either want to move away from an unfulfilling or toxic job or move towards an opportunity which activates us. We either want to cause our teams and organizations to grow, or we maintain the status quo, continually doing things the way they have always been done to avoid the discomfort of change.

Regardless of what it is, there is a paradox involved in change: something needs to end to create space for something else to start. I call this the *"From-To"* and it leads to the question, "What is the decision you're going to make?" Because we do have the personal power to make choices and we can benefit from being intentional about our choices.

With a background that includes decades of changes piled one upon the other rapidly, I was taken aback recently when someone asked me: "At what point did you know it was time for a change?" This made me think, and while I believe it's true that through the practice of reflection and contemplation it's often easier to connect the dots looking backwards than it is to imagine the future looking forward, I also know that change (or growth) is possible in the present moment. I've experienced countless moments of change—some which came as surprises, some through accidents, some by choice, some by heartache, some by opportunity, and others by desire. I've come to learn that change is the result of living in the fluidity of the world. Making choices—practising agency—requires courage. At this stage in my life, I continue to live out the paradox of life, (salsa) dancing between resting and questing, aligning my talents with purpose, living intentionally, and making choices that lead to fulfillment and well-being for myself so I can continue to contribute positively to other people's lives.

A great dissonance may be experienced when change is near: both an old and a new version of yourself might emerge to navigate the change. Unless the change becomes the most dominant vision, you will likely revert to the familiar old. You can't hold two beliefs at the same time without feeling tension (which is the process of dissonance), so it will require openness and risk to keep standing on that ledge of change. This tension is often confused with anxiety, but it's a healthy tension, a way for your mind to indicate to you that there's something new to explore. At this point, you need to decide: *will I take a step forward into the unknown or revert to the known zone?* This is where our decisions lie. Do we pursue a path that requires a great deal of faith (and which involves risk), or do we go back to the way of being we know exists? This type of crossroads often comes out as a signal of fear in our body, but it can also show up as healthy tension. Tension which says, *"I've never seen anything like this before; where will it lead?"* In this place, we require courage and a great leap of faith; it is a place where we choose the unknown. It is a place where we break from ourselves, our habits, and perhaps our family traditions. We might also break from ways that have been ingrained in our way of being through societal expectations and so much more. What will you choose?

THE EVERYDAY LEADER

Remember, there's no right or wrong way of going through change. Let your values guide you. Let your vision fuel your decision.

Several years ago, I was standing at the front of a lecture room at the Sauder School of Business at the University of British Columbia during a personal and professional development class when I had an idea for visually and physically demonstrating the process of change. The students in this class were nearing the end of their studies towards a Master of Management degree and were about to enter a whole new world, a whole new way of living outside of the comforts of student life. They were preparing to enter the workforce, change cities, alter relationships and so much more. I'd like to share this idea and practice with you to help name and move through a process of change.

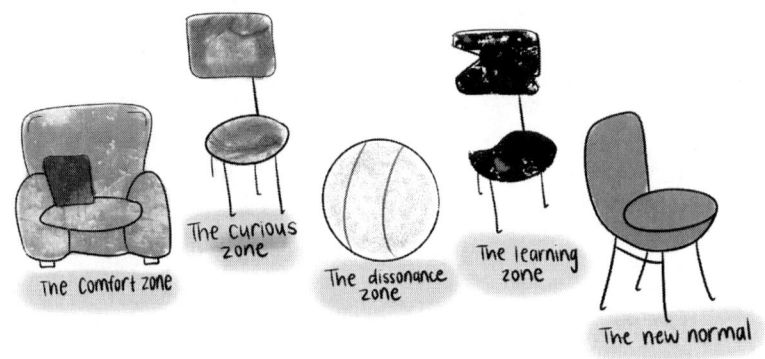

Chair Exercise

Imagine five chairs placed in a room and read on:

- **Chair #1: THE COMFORT ZONE.** You're sitting comfortably, and the chair feels stable and supportive. You may even be sitting on your favourite cushion with your favourite blanket covering your lap and your favourite book nearby. In this zone you know the people around you; you have routine and steadiness. The comfort zone allows you to flow freely and not think too much about everyday tasks. It serves an important purpose in our lives and well-being. In this space, there aren't too many unpredictable issues. You have a general routine, the people around you are steady, your habits are driven unconsciously, and you can count on (for the most part) the fluidity of your daily world, be it at work, home, or while pursuing other scheduled activities and events. In this zone, however, you might start asking questions such as, "what's next?" or "where to from here?"

- **Chair #2: THE CURIOUS ZONE.** This chair is a little wobbly, as if one of the legs is too short or is starting to crack. There's no cushion or blanket, and you're not even sure you should be sitting on this chair. On this chair, you're starting to entertain the idea of change, but you don't want to get off the chair just yet. You are questioning things and may be critically judging yourself. You might be curious about an opportunity for growth or for further study, perhaps taking a leave of absence and exploring a new city, a new relationship, new habits, or something else. This zone is depicted as the zone of curiosity. Curiosity is essential to progress through change, for it is only here that we can create a new world which does not yet exist. In this zone, you might find yourself looking at your current reality with a new perspective, wondering if a change could be the right decision. A lot of questions can arise in this zone. Hence, the wobbly chair and the space of the unknown filled with curiosity about what could be.
- **Chair #3: THE DISSONANCE ZONE.** This chair is not a chair but an exercise ball, and you're standing

on it. Physically, your core is engaged, and you may need help from others to stand on the ball. This is the wobbliest chair of them all, and you know you can't stay on it without support. (Yes, when I demonstrated this in a live classroom, I needed support). Even if you manage to physically get comfortable standing, your brain and emotions are confused, and chaotic thoughts ensue: *should I stay in the comfort or curiosity zone or should I take a leap forward into the unknown?* Again, be aware of your dialogue as the zone of dissonance takes over your thought life. Look inward and figure out what is pulling you—would you like to move away from something, or is something pulling you forward?

- Note: you can always come back here if you're not quite ready yet to address some limiting beliefs at this stage. Ask yourself this: *what's the worst thing that can happen?* You may also recognize that while you might have to let go of some thoughts, you can also choose what you want to carry forward with you, and what is required for you to continue to move through the process of change
- **Chair #4: THE LEARNING ZONE.** Assuming you are ready to take a step forward and embrace the idea of change, you move to the learning zone. This chair is even more wobbly than the second one—it has a broken, leg and the back is missing a piece, but you can still sit on it without crashing to the floor. In this instance, you've decided to move forward with change but are still getting used to the unfamiliar. You're trying to find new rhythms while making new friends and acquaintances. You are familiarizing yourself with your new environment while developing new habits and learning new systems. You are experiencing a sense of unease coupled with hope and curiosity. The hope here is

that you trust yourself. You trust you have chosen a path that best aligns with your true self, the self you explored and can rely on, thanks to the value system which pulled you through Chair #3. This is the learning zone; you're open to growth, you're open to new experiences, and you're in a place of information gathering. The world seems new; it seems fresh, as though there is something still to be discovered in this new normal.

- **Chair #5: THE NEW NORMAL.** You're back in a place of comfort, a new comfort. Getting here took time, patience, and persistence. But you did it. You're comfortably sitting in this chair, but it feels different (in a good way!). Maybe you have a new cushion and a new blanket. Or maybe you just moved the first chair to a different place in the room. Either way, you can settle in here now until the next change comes along.

And that is the story of moving through the process of change. Your thinking might shift to the idea that maybe your normal was so subnormal that you needed a new normal … and the process begins again.

Tolerance for Change

It's worth repeating that *leadership is in the business of repeatedly managing people's transitions.* It's all about the process of giving space to reflect on and answer the hard questions while we manage change. Are you giving space to the grieving process or even acknowledging that it is a process? Some people move through these *chairs* at different speeds and have different needs: we all have different tolerances for the pace of change we can endure at a given time. If there's too much change at once, we may find ourselves or our team members moving into the panic zone or shutting down. On the other end of the spectrum, if there's too little action and change happening, then we also may find people becoming disengaged. So, consider your pace and the pace of those around you; as you aspire to keep people in the learning zone of change, consider where they can move through incremental growth. The tricky part here is that this pace of change will fluctuate depending on the individual, group, or company's moments. Sometimes, we need to increase the pace - raise the challenge and expectations, show contradictions between values and behaviours. At other times, we need to slow the pace and lean into supporting our team members by connecting back to a shared purpose and shared values, providing expertise, bringing people together, and intentionally activating your third ear, masterfully listening to cues in the environment.

Post-Traumatic Growth

So, change happens; we know this and have all experienced it in one form or another. How can change, including traumatic life events, lead to growth? Trauma can be change and change can be traumatic. When you're in the midst of something major—or something minor that feels major—I bet the last thing you are thinking is that the situation you're going through will end up serving you well and will provide an opportunity to be better. Post-traumatic growth includes both negative and positive psychological changes[35].

Let me share with you my story of post-traumatic growth. A few weeks after my divorce was finalized, I was sitting in Mauritius on a lounge chair at an oceanfront six-star resort. I had a moment of rest between facilitating client workshops, so I took the opportunity to pull out a book that had been with me for some time. It was called *Option B* by Sheryl Sandberg and Adam Grant[36]. The concept from this book that stood out the most for me was the idea that *pain can equal purpose*. What? Really? How could this pain I'm feeling from having gone through a traumatic divorce experience ever help me find my purpose? I had put so much of myself into my life in Eswatini, into my relationships, and into things that mattered to me—how could the possibility of it all being taken away be a good thing?

In this moment of reflection on the beach, I took inspiration from that book and began to reimagine what my life *could* be and what it *would* be now that I had chosen a different route forward in my personal life.

- *Who do I want to be?*
- *Why do I exist?*
- *Where do I want to be?*

These three fundamental, powerful questions hit me like a ton of bricks. Do they look familiar from Part 1 of our learning together? Sure, I had thought about these things in my life before, but something about that moment where I reimagined a way forward made it crystal clear m I had to dig deep and find the answers to those questions so I could move on.

My attitude towards life shifted that day. I wanted to learn from my experiences, pave a new path, become the architect of my future, and adopt a mindset of growth. I also wanted to stay flexible and agile enough that I could deal with life's inevitable pivots, twists and turns. Instead of focusing on the hurt and pain, I imagined myself being balanced—checking in on my emotions while also anticipating the future. Although it took a lot of intentional effort and time, I shifted my mindset from being a victim of circumstance to accepting the new reality as it was at that moment. I started taking accountability and carving a way forward; I started to own *my* story and knew I could pivot whenever I wanted to.

As a coach, I take that moment as inspiration to help my clients through transition and change. Even though change can be messy, and it can cloud the mind and confuse your identity, vision, and purpose, it is possible to shift your mindset and reframe the stories you tell yourself. You can move on from ruminating and sensing regret, failure, shame, and guilt to reflecting on your experiences in a different light and being grateful you went through them.

With my own lived experiences and those I help my clients and teams through, I extend the invitation to you to see disruption as an opportunity to grow through your own experience of change and transition.

Reflect to Grow

Change, Transition, Growth

What changes and transitions are you currently experiencing? What might be important for you right now as you give space to both the negative and positive consequences of the experience?

Identify the stage you are experiencing (i.e., which chair are you currently sitting on) and the one your team or organization is experiencing. Ask, "What are we moving towards, or what are we moving away from?" What support do you and your team need to keep moving through the process of change that considers both the hearts and minds of the people involved? Are they similar or different?

What emotions want to be acknowledged as you navigate these changes? What resources can support you—internally or externally?

CHAPTER 17

Workplace Well-being

When we feel well, we perform well. And when we perform well, we feel good, and that matters when you return home from work.

All changes and transitions have an impact on people's well-being and performance. There are costs involved when we do not practice mindful leadership that considers both the complexities of individuals from within and the outer complexities of our fast-paced world: our cultures suffer, and there is also an implication for people's well-being, performance, and attempts to make ends meet. From a workplace perspective, we see turnover, absences, quiet quitting, disengagement, burn-out, and so much more, all of which take enormous tolls on the bottom line and our economies at large[37]. When people suffer due to poor personal or collective leadership, it reminds me of what happens when our body has an infection in one specific location. Toxicity bleeds through our cells and the rest of the body is impacted. The same is true in teams and organizations when people infuse toxic ways of being into their environment: they catalyze or stifle other people's growth and development. What we are talking about here, in particular, is our career well-being and its impact on the economy.

Cost of Disengagement

Our holistic well-being is at risk. A healthy workplace ecosystem matters. Countless leaders I've worked with in recent years are seeing resignations coming in unprecedented numbers. The terms "The Great Resignation" and "Quiet-Quitting" which were coined by Dr. Anthony Klotz, Professor of Management at UCL School of Management, refer to the significant number of employees who were expected to leave their current roles during or towards the end of the COVID-19 pandemic and beyond.

"It's not just about getting another job or leaving the workforce, it's about taking control of your work and personal life, and making a big decision–resigning–to accomplish that," Klotz tells CNBC's *Make It*. "This is a moment of empowerment for workers, one that will continue well into the coming years."[38] Personally, I see this as an opportunity for people moving towards collective agency and stepping into alignment in their career, performance, and well-being journeys.

During the fourth month of the COVID-19 pandemic work-from-home adjustment, I made a change. I had been on the brink of tears, with a lump in my throat for more than a week, unable to manage my workload which was out of the norm for me. A text from my manager sent me over the top. I had said "no" to an additional project request, and my "no" had been completely ignored. My calendar had been jammed with back-to-back meetings for several weeks, and I was hardly able to take a break to eat, let alone run to the bathroom in my 600-square-foot apartment. I had been feeling overwhelmed with the workload with no line-of-sight to a change ahead; it felt like things were going from bad to worse by the week. It was a season where I had learned to set boundaries; I blocked my time, did not answer my phone before or after work, and excused myself from meetings where my presence wasn't mandatory. Yet, the load persisted and continued to escalate. With little recognition and no celebration of the contributions I made, or respect for the load my team was trying to manage, I could hardly keep it together anymore. In that moment, my level of tolerance was depleted, which is unfortunately an all-too-common occurrence in today's world of work

And then this comment came: "Laura, you need some better self-care strategies." I nearly lost it.

I am a person who prides myself on practicing a high degree of personal mastery; I meditate, journal, read, exercise, look after my nutrition, allocate time for spiritual focus and more. I had been managing some chronic digestive issues that had continued to worsen throughout this stressful time. Being isolated during the period of the COVID-19 pandemic, with little-to-no human connection outside of work, certainly did not help. However, what was one more "self-care bath" going to contribute to my well-being at this stage of disengagement, a stage which I ultimately realized was burn-out? The World Health Organization supports that burn-out is a syndrome conceptualized as resulting from chronic workplace stress that has not been successfully managed[39]. What's not clear in this definition is who was responsible for managing the chronic workplace stress.

This had me thinking, at what point is burn-out recognized by an organization, and what role do they play in helping to cultivate healthy workplaces and manageable loads? At what point is it up to the individual to best lead themselves? It is indeed complex. There is a need for multiple layers within an ecosystem to take responsibility for the well-being of people; this is a both/and scenario. The organization is responsible. The individual leaders are responsible. Employees are responsible. As much as we are different, we are all connected in our efforts to move towards well-being.

At the organizational level, we can look to wellness programs and other initiatives. However, if we revisit Gallup's research indicating an employee's direct manager is responsible for seventy percent of their engagement and well-being[40], we must look at the ways in which managers are leading their people. But we cannot ignore the other thirty percent that the direct manager is not responsible for: pressure may be rooted in the organization's strategic plan or in the individuals themselves. It is generally a combination of all of these levels. By exploring unmet employee needs, the manager can have a tremendous impact at the organizational level.

In a post-pandemic world, I recently contributed to an organizational consulting project for a local health authority. No doubt the pandemic caused enormous stress on people of all walks of life, particularly the front-line workers in the healthcare industry and those in leadership positions. We are still recovering and becoming aware of the toll the pandemic has had on our systems—both internally and within the greater world of work. As leaders, we need to be aware of these impacts on ourselves and our team and pay attention to the needs of people who are recovering.

At the individual level, burn-out is also a reflection of how an individual is leading themselves. It is part of a person's responsibility to manage themselves as an adult. Another perspective is that burn-out is a reflection of a person's unmet needs over a prolonged period. These unmet needs can be on a physical level or social-emotional level.

When I looked back and assessed my own strengths/needs paradigm, as well as the invisible identities I was carrying, it was clear what had led to this state of burn-out, and it was the catalyst for yet another change. I went on leave for two months and learned to practice self-compassion. This practice of self-compassion was to be gentle with myself and my narrative while leaning into the truth of my body and offering grace during the period of stress and time off. I rested and calmed my nervous system through a variety of strategies. I then gradually re-integrated into the workplace with a new role which represented an attempt to job-craft my expertise to the needs of the organization. Surprisingly, as a result of my healing and complete rest from work, I felt much better as I stepped into a new department. I felt more aligned, and I felt celebrated and recognized for my unique contributions; I also had a new manager with whom I established a relationship marked by mutual celebration. I was stepping into a growth zone as I felt seen and heard. What was noteworthy about this experience was my own advocacy and growth, as well as the shift I experienced by a change of management that better supported my well-being.

Many clients I've worked with have also expressed similar sentiments, wondering if how they feel relates to the actual role they are in or if it's an expression of their personal well-being journey. The experience of burn-out is real and pressing at the moment; we need to know about it, talk about it, honour it, and encourage each other to protect our well-being so our careers and lives can move to a place of thriving. It is said that in Canada alone, more than 500,000 people are missing work this month (May 2024) due to mental health challenges[41]. Globally, burn-out is on the rise: forty-two percent of the workforce is reporting burn-out, an all-time high since May 2021 when Future Forum started measuring burn-out[42].

Exploring the root of burn-out takes time and a compassionate space held by the individual, the manager, and the organization. It's very difficult to navigate burn-out. In my case, once I went on leave, I also had to manage my narrative about being a perceived failure for taking time for myself. It's certainly obvious from the outside looking in that we need to take care of ourselves before we can serve others. Yet, navigating that process with both internal and external pressures is an undertaking in and of itself. It takes courage to stay true to your values and needs. It really does take all of us: the work we do as individuals combined with management and leadership approaches to ensure well-being is at the heart of people's career well-being journey. Imagine a world where managers have regular check-ins with their employees at a human level on a one-on-one basis—especially during peaks of high stress—in addition to having overall career and holistic well-being conversations with them throughout the year. Managing oneself in order to show up for work at one's best, and breathing hope into an organization's mission, all while navigating the constant flow of change, is exceedingly demanding and continues to challenge our levels of tolerance for change.

Together, we can adopt a new narrative in the workplace: ***to perform well, we must be well.***

Your Career Well-Being

As previously mentioned by Gallup research, those with high levels of career well-being are two times more likely to experience overall well-being in their lives[43]. We also know the motivation for working differs from one person to another. For some, work is about a paycheque: essentially, it's a means to an end. For others, it's about self-development or social connection, or it's about satisfying a calling to contribute, or it's all of those things and more. Regardless of the reason, humans want to feel like their time is valued, their working environments are inclusive, safe, and respectful. They want to know that the teams around them cultivate belonging, that their contributions matter, and that they are encouraged to grow and develop. Ultimately, they want their fundamental needs to be met at a truly individual level within an organizational context.

To help people leaders move to higher levels of career well-being (and mitigate or reduce burn-out) or support your own well-being in the workplace, consider the following elements of the career well-being journey:

1. **Healthy Relationships:** Increased overall well-being includes strong connections and a sense of belonging.

Our relationships with our managers and our peers matter. They help us feel supported, seen, recognized, and appreciated. Hybrid working environments have their pros and cons, but we must not underestimate the significance of purposefully creating moments for people to find connection, belonging, and workplace camaraderie. One of my clients recently returned to work after years of mental health leave and found themselves moving towards thriving simply because they had an authentic relationship with their new manager, who held them both capable and accountable.

2. **Role Clarity:** It surprises me to this day that a very common topic in my individual and team coaching conversations is the lack of clarity around people's roles and the expectations around their performance. As roles change, so do expectations. New hires or shifting organizational charts require a high degree of transparency around who needs to do what and by when. Clear is kind. When role clarity is not pronounced, it is like being lost deep in the forest and taking one step at a time, not sure which direction will lead to the relief of coming out on the other side. No wonder there is uncertainty in the workplace! If someone is deep in a forest with their head down, and they are repeating tasks and managing what comes at them, they can't hope to map out where they are going or find the best way to get there. They are likely to be disoriented and meet only the bare minimum of expectations, all while drowning in demands which seemingly have no purpose.

3. **Boundaries:** People who lead with a strong work ethic and sense of responsibility often move towards burn-out. These people naturally take psychological

ownership of their commitments and even put their hand up for more responsibility than they have the capacity for ("people-pleasers"). They will complete a task or work at all costs, no matter what energy is required ("workaholics"). They are loyal, hardworking and will do what they say they are going to do. Their hunger to work can be exaggerated if they don't honour their work/life and perfectionistic boundaries. This is where burn-out is not about being weak; rather it can also arise from prolonged strength and resilience. What's important with boundaries is that each individual and team has varying degrees of capacity—or windows of tolerance—that they can hold and give to their workplace. Being aware of personal activators (when the bucket is too full) can help people recognize when stronger boundaries need to be exercised.

4. **Growth and Development:** With so many opportunities to grow and develop, it's imperative that people leaders create space to discuss career ambitions and aspirations and act to make them a priority. Otherwise, they risk losing their employees. More recently, I've appreciated the high degree to which managers receive training to become better coach leaders. This is a mandatory skill for leadership in today's workplace, particularly with high-performing individuals.

This skill of using the *Coach-Approach* we've discussed previously requires courage in setting the stage for learning and career conversations so your people can thrive within or outside your team or organization. Trust me, these conversations can actually help you retain people if they see an opportunity to grow and develop! The caveat here is to honour the time and space required to acquire a new skill or take part in training. Consider the pace of people's growth and development, the demands of the workplace, and how those can align. A reminder here is to keep people in the learning zone so they are able to move towards high performance.

5. **Talent Alignment:** In healthy organizations, I have seen leaders who are able to create space to "job craft." This is about identifying people's unique strengths and allowing them to embrace those strengths and interests within roles which also meet the needs of the organization. *Aligning talent with purpose leads to engagement and explicit focus, such as the flow state of performance.* This flow state takes place when both talent and skill development are met with performance challenges. When we're challenging ourselves with a task, our mind reaches full capacity. If the activity at hand happens to be something we enjoy and we're good at it, we achieve a flow mental state — and it can leave us feeling ecstatic, motivated, and fulfilled. If someone is not able to use their natural talents on a daily basis, lack of joy emerges, and then, naturally, an attitude of, "ugh, do I have to do this?" rather than one of, "oh, I love to do this!" will impact long-term performance.

This concept of flow, coined by psychologist Mihaly Csikszentmihalyi, describes a feeling where, under the right conditions, you become fully immersed in what you are doing[44]. The flow mental state is generally less common during periods of relaxation and typically presents during challenging and engaging activities.

We see this flow state a lot when athletes are challenged with the level of competition and demands on their skills that catalyze them to perform at their best, all while managing the anxiety and arousal states that intersect with that level of performance.

In the workplace, when someone is in *the zone,* it shows up when they are fully engaged and feel a manageable level of stress and challenge. If you or your employees are bored, you (or they) will not be performing at the top level of performance available. On the flip side, if our performance anxieties are too high or overwhelming and we aren't able to self-regulate, we freeze, burn-out, underperform, or leave. Individual and people leaders need to maintain a constant state of awareness to both motivate employees and keep them engaged through regular, meaningful conversations about their careers.

There have been times in my coaching career when I've been working with newly hired directors and senior leaders in organizations and found it's taken a while for them to reach the flow state. This might be because they have yet to develop the skill they need or they might perceive the challenge at hand to be too hard, and then anxiety takes over. Contrarily, I've also worked with clients whose pursuit of a title dominated their career move but when they attained that coveted leadership position, they did not enjoy it. This had less to do with their doing and more to do with their being. It's important to have a deep awareness of who you are and what you want to impact in your career. Finding micro-moments of flow, or simply enjoying tasks, is a key factor in creating career well-being and moving to an optimum state.

6. **Embodied Mission**: Knowing and relating to your work's mission impacts career well-being. The topic of purpose fascinates me. It can be a big life question: why am I here? What is my unique contribution to this moment in my career journey? This can be a team or organizational question: why are we here? What are we here to influence? The truth is that your purpose, just like your values, can evolve. We can choose to work for different reasons—a pay cheque, a career advancement, or a calling. Whatever it is for you, as long as you are choosing your work, and it aligns with your talents, then it is valuable.

As people leaders, it's important we continuously remind ourselves about our team's mission or purpose, and also help our team members and employees connect to that purpose. It can be refreshing to look at the macro picture of success and remind people why we do what we do.

Reflect to Grow

Your Career Well-Being Journey

How would you rate your overall experience with your current career?

Looking at the Career Well-being wheel on the following page, what areas are working well for you, and what are some needs that you have to move you closer to thriving in your role?

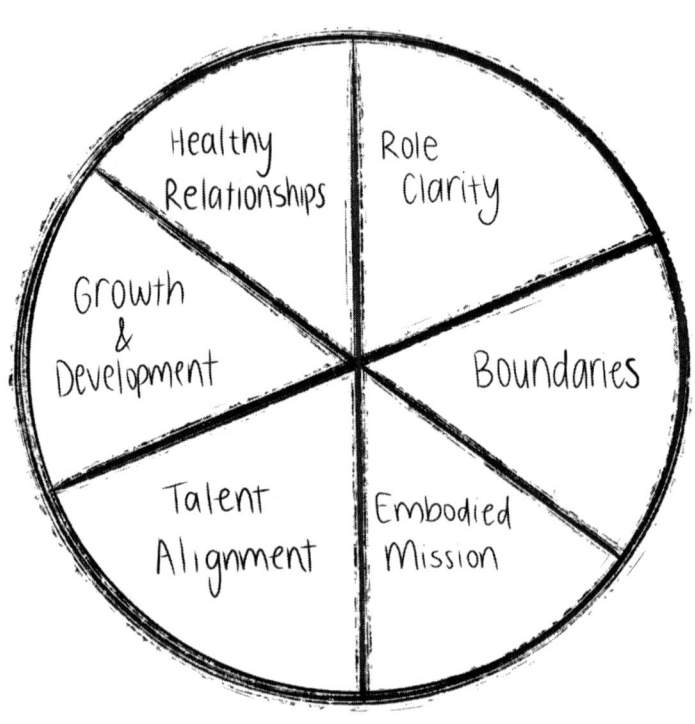

Your Career Well-being

CHAPTER 18

Energy Management

Leadership requires presence and capacity

Everything we say we want in organizations—i.e., engagement, productivity, innovation, connection —first requires human energy, which requires us to explore our own energy and how it impacts our holistic well-being. How we choose to lead and love ourselves from within has an immediate impact on our well-being and the way we show up for others. Our personal leadership impacts the way we engage with others. Being constantly stressed, for example, may hinder our ability to lead well. If we take care of and manage our energy ourselves, we can better hold space for others.

As you take a step closer to being a transformational leader and come full circle to support your efforts and those lives you are impacting, let's give some space to honour your own well-being. This is about you and your energy. It's like putting your own oxygen mask on first in an emergency situation in an airplane so you can better support the people around you. The same is true in your leadership practice, although in this case the "oxygen mask" is about paying attention to and managing your personal energy. Experienced high performers know when to push and when to rest. They know they need to fuel their minds and bodies with the right kind of energy. They know their energy matters. Linking back to Part 1 of this journey, the parts of you outside of your role at work matter, too, like your values and grand visions. This chapter explores what is important for you to consider in your own holistic well-being journey: your energy.

Personal Energy System

As I've shared in previous chapters, I live and advocate for the intentional practices of taking care of the whole self. This includes managing the human body—physically, emotionally, mentally, and spiritually. It's about how we spend our energy in a day: the thoughts we entertain, the books we read, the information (TV, news, social media, etc.) we consume, the people we surround ourselves with, the foods we eat, the ways we rest or don't, the amount of movement we have in a day, and our overall outlook on life. It also includes growing from the inside out, developing agency, confidence and gratitude, and engaging in a continuous exploratory practice of auditing our inner and outer worlds.

I invite you to reflect on your own energy givers and takers by completing the holistic well-being energy audit I've included below. Note: this is an ongoing practice for sustained well-being and performance—try to complete it two or three times per year, if not more.

Holistic Well-Being Energy Audit

All of these components are important at different times and in different phases of your leadership journey. The list below is a starting point and a place of inspiration. You may even create your own list based on the priorities in your life.

Setting all judgements aside, complete your energy hygiene audit. Reflect on what gives you energy and what takes away your energy. For example, some relationships will give you energy, whereas others will leave you feeling depleted. In the case of rest, think about the places, time, and activities that you consider impact your journey. What small changes can you make based on your reflections to give you more capacity to lead well?

	energy givers	energy takers
ENVIRONMENT		
RELATIONSHIPS		
SOCIAL ACTIVITIES		
PHYSICAL WELLBEING		
MENTAL WELLBEING		
EMOTIONAL WELLBEING		
FINANCIAL WELLBEING		
REST		
CREATIVE EXPRESSION		
LEARNING		
CAREER WELLBEING		
LIFESTYLE		
SPIRITUAL PRACTICES		
LEADING AUTHENTICALLY		

Holistic Energy Audit

Rest is Fuel

Do you have the energy you need to get things done? Whatever our current state of health, intentionally managing various forms of rest is necessary for our well-being and represents preventive self-care. In high-performance sports, athletes work on an annual periodization plan that fluctuates between high-stress peaks and low-intensity valleys, so their bodies can integrate the stress of their training. Similarly, at the end of a yoga practice, you enter into a final yoga pose of savasana, "the rest posture," which helps to integrate the benefits of the movements into the muscles and nervous system. In our regular work/life capacities, rest might look and feel different for different people. I encourage you to consider all types of rest if you have been on overdrive lately or want to plan in advance. If we don't make time for rest, our bodies will eventually make time for it. Consider the following components around rest: physical, cognitive, emotional, spiritual, sensory, creative, and social[45].

Perhaps also consider your own boundaries around rest. What are you saying *yes* to when you really want to say *no*? Always being *on* disconnects us from ourselves and from others. Spending time alone, tuning inward, or being outdoors doing something that is rejuvenating and nourishing might allow you to refuel with new energy.

Similarly, when it comes to nutrition and physical activity, our bodies have unique needs and are continuously changing. Moving the body and eating well have immense physical, mental, and emotional benefits, so be sure to commit to what feels good for you.

Mental and Emotional Dimensions of Well-Being

As I have ventured more recently into the world of embodied practices such as yoga and meditation, I've been particularly interested in how emotions and thoughts stored in our bodies can lead to exacerbated physical illnesses. Stress lives in our body and acquires a new home in our cells, which affects our physical well-being[46]. Many researchers and authors, including renowned author and stress expert Dr. Gabor Maté, highlight how our traumas, our pain, or the *dis-ease* of our thoughts impact our physical well-being[47]. Yes, we might assume we have certain genes that are passed down generationally, but it is not the genetic makeup itself that causes addictions or *dis-ease*. It's our behaviours, our environments, our thoughts, our imprinted emotions, and our learned habits which either exacerbate the manifestation of *dis-ease* or keep it at bay.

Emotional literacy is not only valuable in our work performance, but it is also important to our physical well-being. Studying emotions and learning the vocabulary to articulate our emotional world must continue to be at the forefront of our education at home, in school, during sporting activities, and at work, so we can process and protect our physical well-being and move our bodies from suffering to thriving.

Some simple ways you can begin:

- name your emotions; learn the language of emotions to increase your fluency
- embrace the feeling with compassion and curiosity; what might this emotion be trying to tell me?
- lean back into behaviours which align with your values

For example, if you are someone who naturally feels a lot, all the time, you are affected by your own emotional bank and also by those of the people around you. Empathy allows us to connect and feel what others are feeling. In this case, I invite you to consider being intentional about how much emotional energy you have the capacity for in your day-to-day life—as well as how intentional you are in eliminating emotions from your body. Are you able to discern what is yours to keep and what is for the other person to hold on to?

Completing the stress response cycle—the process by which we allow emotions to move through our body and not get stuck in our system—includes being aware of our emotional state, tuning in to the body, and feeling the emotion to get a somatic experience—through intentional mindfulness and breathing work—and then finding ways to let it out[48]. This can be done in many ways including walking, dancing, journaling, laughing, spending time in nature, and devoting time to self-care. While I'm not a therapist or a doctor in the field of epigenetics, I am aware of my body, what its needs are, and who I spend time with. This allows me to keep my emotional bank fully charged, which will then impact my overall physical energy and my ability to be of service.

You might be asking yourself about the role of stress and our well-being. Stress is both good and bad. We've previously discussed how too much stress potentially leads to burnout; however, as mentioned, when we don't have a level of performance anxiety (i.e., feeling bored in our work), the stress required for flow doesn't exist. Flow shows up at the intersection of stress and arousal. However, stress is also bad when there is too much of it and the perceived challenge we are facing is beyond what our bodies can process. Each person has a unique threshold for stress and our window of tolerance alters depending on our makeup, past experiences, and the trauma that lives in our bodies. Our unique wiring must be honoured so stress can exist and at the same time move through our bodies for optimal performance. With this goes the critical concept that periods of stress must also include periods of intentional rest, as we have previously explored, so growth can ensue.

Another way to consider how our mental and emotional well-being intersect is to consider that, "our bodies are eavesdropping on our thoughts," and responding accordingly.

The study of epigenetics suggests exactly this[49]. Our thoughts stir our emotions and then a behaviour follows. Unfortunately, we give up control over much of our lives. We say, "Oh, I was made like this." And while part of that is true, how we think and what we think builds who we are and how we show up in the world. This is control. And we refute it because it's difficult. It's easier to blame others and extend accountability to our friends, our environment, and our upbringing than to fully step into the person we are and the person we want to become. Inner work is the daily practice of living an intentional life. It takes continuous courage, and it requires us to be selective about our thoughts and habits, manage our emotions, and own the process.

Relational Dimensions

Real, authentic relationships are instrumental in the growth and development of human beings. That includes being able to invite those you trust into your world. We are predisposed to be in relationships: through relationships you can observe your own behaviour and that of other people. Relationships are required so we humans can do good work together, laugh and cry together, and experience our full humanity. Developing the muscle of empathy and building relationships, personally and professionally, is intricately connected to our own holistic well-being journey.

Another form of relationship to consider is your relationship to your community or the land on which you live. Community is your connection to the land, people, or spaces where you feel you can thrive. It's instrumental to your sense of joy and ease in life, whether at your workplace, in a community centre, at a religious or spiritual place, in sport, or elsewhere: it's important to consider your community when examining your overall well-being.

Being a good steward of finances can lead to even further fulfillment. I'm just going to be direct and say it. Budgeting and forecasting changed my life and my relationship with money. I was able to be clear about my current reality, all while holding on to the goals I set for myself, including developing greater financial well-being. I started managing my money in a way that works for me. There is so much valuable information out there regarding financial planning, but I lived in a state of lack when I perceived money as a bad or selfish thing. Once I truly accepted that money is abundant, and that it is something which can work in our favour, I changed my relationship with it and what it can generate for my own financial well-being, and those I could help through financial contributions.

When you think about financial well-being, think about how it connects to your purpose and the goals you have set for yourself, and how it can relate to your overall levels of happiness. Happiness can come through spurts of immediate gratification, like a quick purchase online, a tasty meal, or some other transaction that brings an instant response. This is usually short lasting.

When your relationship with money is about satisfying your ego because it helps you feel you have "more than" other people, or you are "better than" others, then you are limiting what is possible in the realm of your financial well-being. Better still is to design your financial management to allow you to give beyond yourselves and contribute to plans for your family, your community projects, your volunteer projects, and other causes that are bigger than yourselves.

Mindset Matters

Personal energy also includes having a mindset that seeks unlocked potential, an optimistic lens for the future, and uncovering what finding personal fulfillment truly means for you within your own mind and heart so you can generously extend that to others.

Through a plethora of lived accidents in sport and life, I've learned there are tools and life skills that are foundational to building the muscle of resilience. One of the tools that transformed my life was visualization. The first time I learned about visualization was after I tore my anterior cruciate ligament (ACL), which is a ligament in the knee which keeps the shin bone and the thigh bone aligned. During my rehab days, I sat with a sports psychologist and studied the image of a healthy ACL, one which was securely attached and whole. If our bodies are eavesdropping on our every thought, wouldn't it be valuable to make sure our thought life was a true reflection of the way we wanted our body to be and function?

Since then, I have used the idea of visualization to not only recover from pain but to use vision to create a future which does not yet exist. Your life is going to move in the direction of your most dominant thoughts, so be careful what you think, because what you think about the most will grow!

Let me share with you another time when my life got flipped and turned upside down and how I went through a season of repair.

Early one day while I was still living in Southern Africa, a friend asked me to join him and his family on an afternoon bike ride through trails I had yet to explore. His wife and kids were meeting us at the actual park whereas he and I decided to ride there instead of driving since not all the bikes would fit in the car. We set off. I noticed right from the start we were cycling faster than I was used to, though with me and my adventurous spirit, I tried to keep up on my borrowed bicycle. Less than 300 metres into a ride that was abundant with irregular potholes and full of twists and turns, I noticed my friend was up ahead, just barely out of sight. Moving at quite a speed now, on a slight downward slope, I encountered a small ledge on the path. The next thing you know I'm being taken to the hospital. My friend's wife had arrived on the scene minutes after I fell to find me unconscious. Other than my right leg, which was kicking sporadically, my body showed no indication of being alive.

My helmet had saved my life.

The process that unfolded thereafter had me thinking about many things, including the choices I had made in my life. It was a key moment to learn from and reflect upon.

Yes, accidents happen…but what had I been trying to prove to myself or my friend? What unconsciously drove my behaviour that day? What was the pain I was running from? Where was I trapped and what was my body wanting to express?

Why didn't I go slower or ask to test-ride the bike a little bit more before going full throttle? What was the need to keep up about? Even though I chose this adventure, I still had fears when the speed exceeded my norm.

The first hospital I was in was quite reputable, however, after medical staff spent several hours trying to clean the rocks, pebbles, and gravel out of the right side of my face, which had been torn open in the accident, they decided I should either be taken across the border with a helicopter for plastic surgery or moved to another hospital for a CT scan. It's all a bit of a blur and certainly, I was in enough shock that it helped numb the pain for some hours. But locking eyes (with the one eye that was not entirely swollen shut) with my friends and my husband at the time, was enough to tell me things weren't looking good. I remember trying to stand up to use the washroom at one point and fell right back down again. I could hear whispers on the side, "Okay, so who is going to pay for this?" "What do her finances look like? Who can chip in?" – we needed to pay for my hospital visit and I knew very well I had less than a few dollars in my bank account. And no medical insurance.

The Pain Had Started to Surface

Soon after I was packed into an ambulance across the city to another hospital about an hour's drive away. The driver was going way too fast, and I mumbled for him to go slow. The pain had started to surface, and I was not well.

The waiting game continued and at this point now, one of my dearest friends—who was also at the time my manager at work—arrived. She took one look at me (picture my head wrapped up like a mummy with one eye visible) and all her expressions spoke volumes. The words that came out of her mouth were, "What's your self-talk like? Pull yourself together, we are supposed to go to New York in three weeks."

"Right," I thought, "it can't be that bad," though I just wanted to burst into tears as I *couldn't* hold it together anymore. I was weak. I was vulnerable. I had no idea where I was, or what was going on, though I had people: people who cared, people who showed up, people who showed me in their faces that everything was going to be okay even if nobody knew for sure. Turns out my friends at the time were having meetings that involved statements like, "What the flip are we going to do?" outside of my room but were rosy and smiley when entering my vicinity, showering me with words of care and comfort. Ah, friends, I'm forever amazed by their generous and loving spirits.

So, it turns out I had no internal bleeding, and after some further cleaning up, which required many needles full of anesthetic to numb my face so staff could clean the dirt and stitch me up again, and a few nights in the hospital, I was sent home. My friends became my full-time caregivers; I even moved in with a friend who took care of me during those first few days. It was Christmas and I was just glad to be able to slurp some chia water through an opening on the right side of my mouth. I even attempted to suck on a piece of chocolate. Oh, what a treat! But that was it.

It took a few weeks for the skin on my face to miraculously heal, and then I was back at work and ready to pack my bags for New York City about a month later. I had healed quickly on the outside and it seems wild now, thinking about it, to recognize how incredible our bodies are.

My self-talk and visualization practices were at their best. I remember repeatedly visualizing the image I had of myself thanks to the most recent headshot we had taken of me for the business. I clearly visualized my face whole and healed. My friends were incredibly supportive throughout this whole process! Yet, what was happening inside of me took many months—years, even—to process. *Our scars, whether on the outside or deep inside of us, are part of our story.* Some are visible, some are not, yet we persevere as we heal and grow from strength to strength…as long as we have the right support, and our needs are met.

Imagine a world where you feel seen and heard, both that part of you that is visible to the eye and that which might not be apparent at first.

The moment of this accident was yet another catalyst for change. I started making decisions that were better for my health and my family. I was getting used to a new body, walking gingerly forward. I had trouble being exposed to sunlight for many months after the accident and I came to accept the scarring on my face. While all this happened externally, something more was happening internally.

My self-awareness heightened. What's most important to me right now? I started questioning my choices, my life, my well-being, and my future. What was I doing? Who was I spending my time with? My work relationships grew closer. My manager, who was also the CEO of the company I had just joined, was my anchor. She knew what I needed. That is a significant human quality needed in the 21st-century workplace. Though I may not have needed to jump on a flight halfway across the world, I did need a vision. I needed to imagine myself whole and well. Some nights she called me to chat. Other nights she prayed with me. We continued to build a business. We used the story of the power of my visualization, again and again, sharing it with leaders about the power of vision. I think more than this, she was an incredible human to meet me where I was, care for me like a friend, and continue to inspire my professional journey for years to come. *Vision, indeed, gives pain a purpose.*

There are choices to follow and choices to lead all around us. On a bike course, in our relationships, friendships, community, cultures, and so much more. After the accident, I started to choose, intentionally and carefully. I started to express my needs. Accidents have a funny way of letting us know our voices are not being heard.

The cost of not making intentional choices as leaders is that we repeat our habitual ways of being. Without changing course, or examining our truth, we simply live by default in a setting that has been conditioned in our subconscious mind and where our belief systems, expectations, habits, and mindsets have been moulded since childhood. Some beliefs are automated and serve us well; those are the ones which have, for example, gotten you this far. Others have caused fear, self-doubt, and criticism. These are the narratives limiting your ability to move through areas of stuck-ness and/or show up as a leader who is empowering instead of one who causes fear or harm. Pay attention to those as they are limiting your ability to achieve your potential and any goals that support its actualization.

We can identify anything that has become automated in our belief system through our behaviours. Are there triggers causing you to react which in turn causes harm to others? Is there a pattern in your life where you are the common denominator? For example, do you find yourself in repeated conflicts with colleagues, no matter what team you're on? If yes, this is your cue to pause and examine what is at the root of that behaviour and then intentionally reprogram it through healing practices and the art and science of neuroplasticity.

Contemplative Practices
Intention and attention are at the heart of human development

In a world rife with information overload, we are starved for presence. Presence to connect with our own hearts and minds, and with others. It's putting the concept, *slowing down, to speed up*, into practice.

As you observe yourself reading further, start to simply notice. Notice where you're sitting or standing. Notice the ground beneath your feet or the feeling of being supported by a chair. Notice if you are tense or relaxed. Notice if your jaw is clenched or you're frowning. Notice the light filtering into your space. Notice the sounds around you. Notice any smells or tastes that linger in your senses. As you begin to notice, start to observe your breath. There's no need to change it or fix it, simply become aware. Notice the temperature of the air entering through your nostrils. Notice if it changes when you exhale.

Now, if you can increase your inhale through your nose (into your belly, rib cage and lungs) and exhale just a little bit longer, I invite you to do so. Try counting, and increasing both the inhale, pause, and exhale. For example, inhale for the count of 4, hold for the count of 7, and exhale for 8. Once you've done a few rounds, gently release, and return to your regular rhythm of breathing. What do you notice? How does your body feel? Simple breathing exercises are a powerful way to ground yourself, to notice where you are holding energy, and to remind yourself of your full humanness. Where your breath goes, energy flows.

It is a slight shift in focused attention. Stop and take a breath before replying to a text; switch the hand you use to regularly brush your teeth, feel the bristles brush up against your teeth or swirl the mouthwash an extra few seconds; when you get into your car, take a moment to feel your body touching the seat or notice the smell before you turn on the engine; as you go to bed, take a moment to give thanks for the day; smell your food before you eat mindfully, and please, try not to multitask!

Mindfulness practices help build the muscle of focus, the capacity to pay attention, the opportunity to rewire neural pathways, improve emotional intelligence, and so much more. There are many centring and contemplative practices such as mindfulness meditation, breathwork, visualization, writing, and journaling activities (such as expressing gratitude) that I invite you to consider in your embodied leadership journey. It's a fascinating time for leaders who are willing to learn, unlearn, and relearn, to dive deeper into contemplative practices and use them to live out their authentic embodied leadership aspirations.

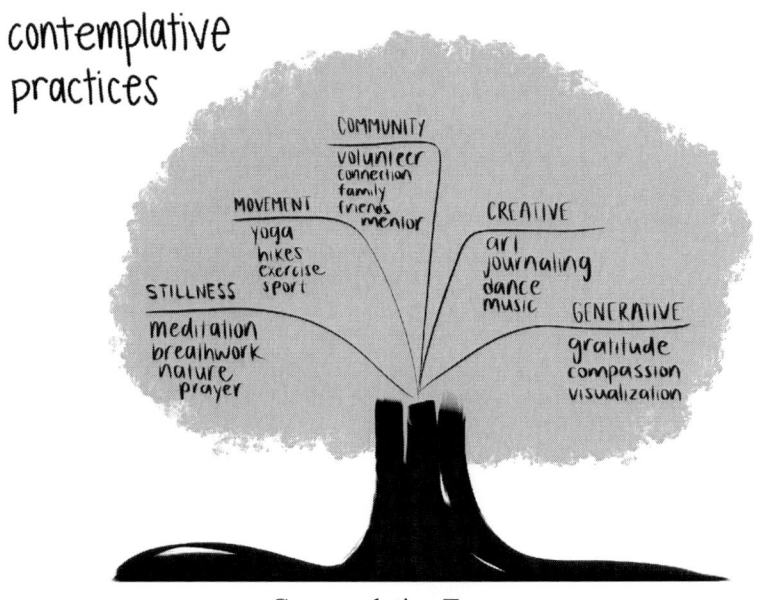

Contemplative Tree

Contemplative Practices

What are your go-to contemplative practices where you find your breath, your grounding, your centering? Consider what difference they make to your overall well-being journey. How can you be even more intentional with them?

CHAPTER 19

What's Love Got to Do with It?

Leadership is love in action.

As I conclude this journey with you, I wanted to share the moment that surprised me, beyond any textbook, training, sports arena or workplace experience; the story of Nothando. This incredibly potent part of my story has taught me about resilience and shaped who I am—as a leader and as a human being—and what came to be the heart of leadership. The story stems from my relationship with one child, one gift that has led to my journey of self-actualization. It amazes me that one emotion has the power to make such a dramatic change in one's life. And it has made all the difference in mine.

Agape
In the Zulu and Siswati languages, the name Nothando means love. This is the story of a girl named Nothando who came into my life several years ago. Nothando changed my life.

It was a Sunday morning, the hot African sun was on the rise, and I was warming up for a friendly tennis match with a friend at the local resort hotel. Hotels were the place to swim, to get a bit of leisure, to play golf, and enjoy a Western-style meal. They were nestled throughout the country in the rolling hills of the Kingdom of Eswatini. We were mid-volley when my phone rang. It didn't just ring once–you know the ring you just want to ignore. No, the phone kept ringing and ringing and ringing, so I apologized for interrupting the game when I went to answer the call; I scrambled to find the phone I had tucked into my backpack.

I heard the desperation in my ex-husband's voice as he said, "Please can you come to the village right away, I need you here." I don't remember much between the phone call and my entering the village less than a twenty-minute drive away. The village's red clay roads are filled with foot-deep potholes, usually on both sides of the road, and there was generally only enough space for one car coming in either direction—so even if I had wanted to speed, there was just no way I could. I parked under an acacia tree, for the sun was close to peaking, and I would be glad of shade on a day like this.

An air of stillness, of thick emotion, greets me as I enter the grandmother's traditional African home, known as a *rondavel*. I lock eyes with my ex, see his sisters and his son and a few other small children, relatives who lived under the same roof. The usual laughter, hugs, and dancing energy I had been accustomed to in this space are neither seen nor felt. To my left, I see a child lying curled up and almost numb, not moving, on a sofa bed. She is wearing a dress, a bit torn up, that probably could use a wash, or could even be thrown in the bin. I pause, trying to process and catch up on the vibe, the air, and the confusion in the dark room. The beauty of these rondavel-style homes is that their thatched roofs keep them cool—something that is much needed in the sunny summer.

I get back to locking eyes with my ex and lean in. "Sorry, what's happening?" I ask. He always spoke with a softness in his eyes, and he had a heart of gold. He says, "Well, this is Nothando." He nods his head in the direction of the child lying on the sofa. "She is my child, and she has been abandoned by the grandmother of the mother. She was living with the grandmother, and the mother had disappeared out of town or country a few months back, and, well, this morning she was dropped off here with nothing more than a crinkled old shopping bag with an old toothbrush and two pieces of clothing inside. They all needed to be washed or thrown away because of the state they were in."

I take a deep breath. At this point in our relationship, we had separated, and I was living away from our marital home. We had endured a year full of unhappy events and heartaches. Even so, human nature—the fight or flight stress response—kicked in. My sense of responsibility kicked in. The nurturing compassionate woman inside me kicked in.

I look at him fiercely. I don't think I know all the emotions I was feeling at the time and what came out of my mouth was this next thought, "So what are *you* going to do (and why am *I* here)?" I knew my role as a friend, a wife, a stepmother and a human being was to show love and show up for people who needed me the most. He said, "Well, I'm going to take care of her every day for the rest of my life." I said, "Okay, well, let's go." I had a car to transport them to our home away from the village, which meant we would take Nothando and my stepson, a boy not my own who called me, "Mom."

As my ex went to pick up Nothando, she refused to go with him. There was no way this child was going to let a male figure pick her up. Once again, there was a lapse in time. I can't remember what happened but within seconds of my ex trying to pick her up and her refusing, Nothando nestled herself over to me as I was now sitting next to her on the couch, and she wrapped herself around me like a koala. Her legs were bowed due to severe malnourishment, also known as rickets, and their curvature allowed for an extra tight grip around me. She flung her arms around me. I had never felt this kind of connection before. It was a child's way of calling out for love, belonging, connection, safety, and comfort, for all the things a two-and-a-half-year-old child should get in every moment of their existence. It was the kind of hug that meant, "Please take care of me." And I didn't hesitate for a second.

What Does a Child Need?

I passed the next few hours in response mode. Okay, what does a child need? We drove to the grocery store, to a clothing store, to the pharmacy, and straight home. Nothando waited in the backseat of the car for me to pick her up and take care of her. Before entering the home, while holding tightly to this God-given child, I stood still for a moment. I looked at my ex and his son, and I said this. "This sister, this child here, needs two things. She needs love and she needs food. Promise me with all your might, you will love this child."

She clung to me every minute from then on in. I demonstrated what a toilet was, how it works, and where to find running water—yes, it comes from the tap over the sink. Yes, there is a bathtub in which we can run water and you can bathe in warm water. By this point, I had been living in Eswatini for at least four years, but I had never spoken the native language enough to have a conversation with anyone. Well, that changed overnight. I suddenly needed to learn a language, to communicate with a child I had fallen in love with, to care for, to nurture her, like she was my own. Nothando loved yogurt and her new water bottle. She loved her doll and the koala-bear-style wraparound way she latched on to me. She only ate when I was present, she was not to be left alone. I felt bad in a way that her dad could not touch or be close to her, although this developed over time.

The next few days were a blur. I must have spent several hours a day at the clinic with Nothando getting all sorts of tests done. One afternoon, after a long wait in the waiting room, I began to feel uncomfortable being the only white woman surrounded by the opinions and assumptions of black families (I heard many times "Oh, there's an Umlungu – a white woman"). But those interjections didn't matter anymore. What mattered was this child's health. So, we waited and saw several doctors to get advice on her malnourished body and the deformation of her legs. She had been abused by what local people would refer to as the witch doctors. They believed the deformation of her legs was the work of evil spirits (not a lack of love or emotional support). She had scars on every one of her joints, she had been taken to these "doctors" and they had made micro-cuts on her to "heal" her legs. I don't know the details and didn't ask more. Maybe one day I'll learn more about their practices. Late in the afternoon, we were now getting ready for some injections. This was a piercing moment for me. As the nurse asked me to hold on tight to Nothando and moved in to give her an injection, Nothando screamed at the top of her lungs, "Mama, Mama, I want my Mama." My heart melted. I cried holding this child who was living in fear. I cried because I was not her mama, yet I loved her like she was my child. I wished her mom was there to care for her.

Selah. Pause. Breathe.

> ***Breathe…the Essence of Life***
> ***Rise and Fall…the Rhythm of Life***
> ***Peaks and Valleys…the Journey of Life***
>
> ***Love…all there is to Life***
>
> —*Michelle Lee*[50]

So, what's love got to do with it? It's everything. Nothando's story is one of bravery, resiliency and love. Her name even means love, so that is what she shall receive. This is where the concept of *Agape* comes in. Agape, or altruistic love, means having unconditional love for all beings. Nothando is the mightiest, smartest and most strong-willed child I have ever met. As I write this book, she is just shy of age twelve and she is at the top of her class. She has straight legs, her teeth are growing well, and she is a force in her own home.

My reflections on the story of Nothando and the other thousands of inspirational resiliency stories around the world have shaped my outlook on life and leadership. How do our decisions impact the way we lead our lives, our families, our communities, our businesses and the world? How is it possible we have the power to choose: to choose love over fear; love over hate; life over death? Yet, again and again, we see pain inflicted–consciously or unconsciously—on people in our everyday lives. We also see joy, the expression of creativity, engagement, love, and excitement, as a result of practicing authentic and embodied leadership.

The decision to live intentionally and authentically—or not—is yours to make.
There are no shortcuts. There are no magic bullets to ensure we show up as the best person who represents our higher self. But we do have a choice. Having agency means you are taking back your power to sit in the driver's seat of your life and your transformational leadership practice. You are a leader. You have the ability to make a positive change in your life and those around you. How will you continue to lead with love?

Reflect to Grow

Your Leadership Legacy—Work, Home, Community
Develop a Leadership Philosophy, considering ME–WE–US, include all the parts. Write a letter as your future self about your leadership philosophy. What parts of you want to be expressed in your leadership practice? What will anchor and guide the contributions you want to make to the world? What do you want to be remembered for? And, who do you want to impact?

CONCLUSION

Our world is certainly evolving by the minute. It's time to be courageous about your leadership journey and to create space for alignment with your most authentic self. It's time for your inner world (your being) to catch up with your outer world (your knowing) and experience the world of work and living in a way that is fulfilling, sustainable, and supportive of your individual needs. This is something artificial intelligence cannot replace: the human heart and mind.

When you are not growing, you are not evolving.

This exploration requires agency, and it is for all of us to grasp, hold on to, develop, and know it's possible for you to navigate complex challenges. I hope this book has instilled belief in you, that it reminds you that the better you lead yourself, the stronger your relationships will be, and the greater the impact you will have as you aspire to a better tomorrow. In these times, it rings true that people most need us to lead with *hope*.

I don't have all the answers to your complex challenges. When I think about the world today, there is much to be grateful for in the advancement of human development. However, there is more work to be done, one conversation at a time. Knowing is one thing, taking action is another: that's why it's a *practice*.

The clients I work with, both the young and the seasoned, are prepared for the challenge, and that is why I celebrate them—and you—in their journeys of advancing the human condition through their leadership journey. When we start to ignite the curiosity of self-discovery and the decision to make different choices, it's never easy. This work is hard. This work on the inside might scare you and be foreign to you. You might not like what you find and then *that* becomes your work. The replacement picture on the other side, though…this is where you find freedom. Free will. The freedom to choose. And true being, true love, exists when there is a choice.

Ultimately, this book is an invitation into your own leadership, your growth and your development, so you can positively impact those you influence–at home, at work, in sport, and in your communities.

Personal and professional development is a dynamic process of action, reflection on that action, and then new and more effective action in light of the new information gleaned. This is a continuous process, and it is the key to increasing leadership effectiveness for collective thriving and impact.

You hopefully have by now come to appreciate that the process of leading from within is a practice of continued self-discovery. The value of honing your own leadership practice creates the positive conditions for the people you lead to thrive. If leadership is about enabling, we must dare to enable ourselves to start with exploring and aligning the system within, so we can hold space for others and create thriving systems between us. As a leader—formally or informally—your practice, the way in which you choose to know yourself, stay anchored in your values, and align your authentic way of being to the world, is the joy of the exercise. It's not a finite game. We change. We grow. We repeat the process of moving ourselves and our people through change and transition. The choice is with us; do we choose to reflect and grow or stay and repeat? If we don't change, we stay stuck.

This process of change involves a push-pull dynamic. Neither is good nor bad; however, it is for us to choose which best positions us to fulfill our potential and unlock our human power. Change on the inside (as well as on the outside) is the precursor to our evolution so we can tap into our humanness and experience life to the fullest; it serves us well to recognize when we are stuck and when we are ready to make intentional choices. One thing is for certain: I have now come to settle on the fact that *you can either have comfort or you can have growth, but you can't have both at the same time.* We have seasons of comfort and seasons of growth. They inform each other. I invite you to consider where you are staying stuck in your leadership comfort and what awaits you as you explore growth opportunities, both personally and professionally.

So, whether you are learning to take agency and lead yourself, and lead others—at home, in the workplace, or on the sports field—authentic leadership is available for you to pursue. We can choose what we believe in and the impact we want to have on ourselves and others by living our values, and by practicing responsible leadership so our collective well-being is at the forefront of a new normal. By investing in ourselves, reflecting, engaging in deep contemplative practices, and looking inward, we can become everyday leaders who make a positive impact on people's lives and development.

The world is counting on it.

GLOSSARY

Authentic Leadership: Authentic leadership is a leadership style that emphasizes genuineness, self-awareness, and transparency in one's interactions with others. Authentic leaders strive to align their actions, values, and beliefs, demonstrating consistency between what they say and what they do. By modelling authenticity and integrity, authentic leaders create environments where individuals feel valued, supported, and motivated to contribute their best.

Agape: A Greek term often used to describe a form of love that is unconditional, selfless, and compassionate. It represents the highest form of love, altruistic love, a universal kind of love for humanity.

Burn-out: Burn-out is a syndrome conceptualized as resulting from chronic workplace stress that has not been successfully managed.

Coach-Approach: A style of communication for leaders to engage with workplace relationships that demonstrate both care and stimulates personal responsibility.

Collaboration: Meaning to co-labour, to do good works together in pursuit of a common goal.

Ecosystem: A complex network or interconnected system of people interacting in a common environment.

Emotional Intelligence (EI): The key to both personal and professional success. EI is the capacity to be aware of, control and express one's emotions, and to handle interpersonal relationships judiciously and empathetically.

Emotional Capital Report: A psychometric tool that signifies an innovation in the measurement of leadership behaviours. It is an exciting advance in our ability to measure the building blocks which are scientifically linked to the behaviours of successful leaders.

Fulfillment: A feeling of happiness, satisfaction of achievement, contentment.

Gallup CliftonStrengths™: An assessment that identifies your unique talents—your natural patterns of thinking, feeling and behaving. It also includes resources to help you understand what you do best and how to use your talents to live your strongest life.

Leadership: The action of leading a group of people or an organization. This includes getting people to confront and deal with problematic realities on behalf of improving the human condition.

Learning Zone: Nestled between your comfort and panic zone. It is the sweet spot of performance; the place where you experiment, develop skills and stretch your abilities.

Mental Fitness: Indicates your ability to think clearly and to make decisions effectively and efficiently through deliberative awareness of your thought life.

Metanoia: A term derived from Greek that generally refers to a profound change in one's thinking, perspective or way of life. It encompasses a transformative shift in consciousness, beliefs, values, or behaviour, often characterized by a deep sense of repentance, self-reflection, and personal growth. Metanoia implies a fundamental reorientation of one's mindset or worldview, typically leading to a more enlightened or evolved understanding of oneself and the world.

Mindfulness: A mental state characterized by focused awareness and non-judgmental observation of the present moment, including thoughts, feelings, bodily sensations, and the surrounding environment. It involves deliberately paying attention to experiences as they arise, without getting caught up in past regrets or future worries.

Practicing mindfulness often involves techniques such as meditation, breathing exercises, or simply being fully present in whatever activity one is engaged in. By cultivating mindfulness, individuals can develop greater clarity, emotional resilience and overall well-being.

Playing Field: A metaphor of your team's ecosystem and Ways of Working; a strategy for team success.

Personal Mastery: The deliberate practice of taking care of the whole self.

Post-traumatic growth: The positive psychological change some individuals experience after a life crisis or traumatic event.

Psychological Safety: A workplace consideration whereby people have the belief they won't be punished or humiliated for speaking up with ideas, questions, concerns or mistakes.

Responsible Leadership: Demonstrates values-based leadership, personal development and an understanding that sustainability is key to long-term success.

Sawubona: A Zulu greeting that translates to "I see you" in English. It carries a deeper meaning beyond just acknowledging someone's presence; it conveys respect, recognition, and a sense of interconnectedness.

Selah: It is thought to prompt reflection, meditation, or a moment of silence to contemplate the preceding text. Its usage suggests a pause for the listener to consider the significance of what was just said or sung.

Strengths/Needs Paradigm: A philosophy supporting the idea that when someone's strengths and needs are identified and expressed, it can help an individual or a manager best leverage performance, engagement, and well-being.

Team Culture BluePrint™: A development tool that provides feedback on your team's current mindset, providing leaders with a baseline to target continuous growth toward enhanced future performance.

Thriving: The state of flourishing or prospering in various aspects of life. It encompasses not only material success but also emotional well-being, personal growth, and fulfillment. When someone is thriving, they are experiencing overall positive outcomes in their health, relationships, work, and personal development. Thriving individuals often exhibit resilience, adaptability, and a sense of purpose, allowing them to navigate challenges effectively and find joy and satisfaction in their lives.

Third Ear: A term used to describe generative listening—listening beyond the words of what someone is trying to say.

Transition: A process or period of change from one state, condition or situation to another. It can encompass a wide range of shifts, including changes in personal circumstances, life stages, social roles, or organizational structures. Transitions can be gradual or sudden, planned, or unexpected, and they often involve adjustments, adaptations, or transformations in behavior, beliefs, or environment.

Ways of Working: Established and agreed upon behaviours that govern the aspirational values of a group or team of people working together.

Well-being: Not merely the absence of illness or distress but rather a holistic sense of thriving and flourishing. Factors which contribute to well-being include good physical health, positive emotions, a sense of purpose and meaning in life, fulfilling relationships, a supportive social network, and a feeling of accomplishment and satisfaction. Achieving and maintaining well-being involves nurturing these different aspects of life and striving for a balanced and fulfilling existence.

Values: The fundamental beliefs and principles that guide an individual's attitudes, behaviours, and decision-making. They represent what is important and meaningful to a person, shaping their priorities and influencing their actions in various aspects of life.

Ubuntu: "Ubuntu" is a Nguni Bantu term originating from Southern Africa. It is often translated as "humanity towards others," or "I am because we are." Ubuntu embodies a philosophy that emphasizes the interconnectedness of humanity and the importance of community, compassion, and mutual support. It underscores the idea that individuals exist within a network of relationships and that their well-being is intricately linked to the well-being of others. Practicing ubuntu involves showing empathy, respect, and kindness towards others, fostering a sense of belonging and solidarity within society. It is deeply rooted in African traditional values and has gained recognition as a guiding principle for social harmony and collective development.

ABOUT THE AUTHOR

Change-driven, growth-minded, and hope-filled.

Laura Dowling is a globally recognized transformational leadership coach who brings energy and passion to her work assisting Olympians, business leaders, students, and others who have heard the siren call of a greater future. She brings a strategic grace to her purpose-driven work igniting individual and team success in clients' lives, drawing on an international sporting career as well as academic studies in sociology, psychology, and population health. Her goal is to bring her clients the most impactful and inspiring support possible; her results speak for themselves.

As the founder and principal consultant of LD Performance Consulting, a boutique holistic leadership development enterprise, she provides customized solutions to companies around the world. Her expertise has contributed to the success of various industries and thousands of individuals in almost all areas of work: corporate, private, and public sectors, higher education, tech, healthcare, high performance sport, non-profit, and faith-based organizations.

Laura is a coach, trainer, consultant, and mentor, and a sports, yoga and meditation enthusiast. Her life is the culmination of global projects across three continents that have provided her with a rich variety of experiences. Each adventure, from the valleys of heartache and grief to the joy and achievement of summiting mountain tops and visiting awe-inspiring wonders of the world, have contained unexpected treasures that have shaped her understanding and perspective of the world around her.

To work or collaborate with Laura through your adaptive leadership challenges, find ways to engage through her website ldperformanceconsulting.com.

ACKNOWLEDGEMENTS

Writing a book is both a mirror and a window. It is the reflection of experiences I've had the privilege to live and be a part of. I'd like to extend a heartfelt gratitude to my family for the daughter who couldn't wait to get out into the world and continue to explore her identity beyond the confines of a family unit. To my sister, Melissa, who gets to edit my work regularly and is a champion of my own agency. My eternal thanks to the souls who have shared their inner world with me.

To both my editors Susan Crossman and Sophia Faria for creating space to translate my lived experiences to writing, structuring, editing, and being key contributors to unlocking my creative spirit in putting words to paper. Also, for the immense patience and energy to gently support and nudge this project along over several years.

I'd like to acknowledge past researchers, teachers, mentors, authors whose work has influenced the world of coaching and human development and inspired me to pursue this field of work. To my colleagues and friends who have asked me hundreds of times, "when is your book ready?" -I see you and feel your unconditional support.

Thank you to Lipika Grover for contributing your creative illustrations and being a champion of growth and change; Michelle Lee for your wisdom and offering to have me share your poetry.

I also recognize that my place of privilege in the world allows me to exercise agency intentionally in the service of others; externally through travelling, moving, and exploring the far corners of the world, and inwardly through deep introspection and the recognition which comes from drawing on the lessons resident in painful truths and experiences. It is in these wonders of the world, literally and figuratively, that I am inspired to live, move and be.

ENDNOTES

1. Rath, Tom. StrengthsFinder 2.0. Gallup, 2017.
2. Kalchman, Lori. "Making NHL a Very Long Shot." Hockey Canada. Last modified 2003. https://www.hockeycanada.ca/en-ca/news/2003.
3. O'Brien, Tom. "When Your Job Is Your Identity, Professional Failure Hurts More." Harvard Business Review, 2019.
4. Williams, Serena. "Serena Williams Says Farewell to Tennis On Her Own Terms—And In Her Own Words." As told to Rob Haskell. Photography by Luis Alberto Rodriguez. Styled by Gabriella Karefa-Johnson. Vogue, August 9, 2022.
5. Reuters. "Roger Federer to Retire from Tennis After Next Week's Laver Cup." Reuters, September 15, 2022. Last updated September 16, 2022. https://www.reuters.com/sports/tennis/roger-federer-retire-tennis-after-next-weeks-laver-cup-2022-09-15/.
6. Clifton, Donald O., and Jim Harter. Wellbeing at Work: How to Build Resilient and Thriving Teams. Gallup, 2021.
7. Buckingham, Marcus. Love and Work: How to Find What You Love, Love What You Do, and Do It for the Rest of Your Life. Harvard Business Review Press, 2022.
8. Grant, Adam. What Frogs in Hot Water Can Teach Us about Thinking Again. TED, 2021.
9. Hernandez, Angie Orellana, and Amy Haneline. "Will Smith Slapped Chris Rock at the 2022 Oscars. Here's What Has Happened Since." USA Today, April 6, 2022. https://www.usatoday.com/story/entertainment/celebrities/2022/04/06/will-smith-chris-rock-2022-oscars-what-happened-since/123456789/.
10. Kahneman, Daniel. Thinking, Fast and Slow. Farrar, Straus and Giroux, 2011.
11. Williamson, Marianne. Live in Vancouver: Evolve Together. 2022.

12 Gallup. "History of CliftonStrengths." Gallup. Last modified 2024. https://www.gallup.com/cliftonstrengths/en/253754/history-cliftonstrengths.aspx#ite-254129.
13 Chamine, Shirzad. Positive Intelligence: Why Only 20% of Teams and Individuals Achieve Their True Potential and How You Can Achieve Yours. Greenleaf Book Group Press, 2012.
14 Positive Psychology. Seligman's PERMA+ Model Explained: A Theory of Well-Being. 2017.
15 Kaufman, Scott Barry. Transcend: The New Science of Self-Actualization. Tarcher Perigee, 2020.
16 García, Héctor, and Francesc Miralles. Ikigai: The Japanese Secret to a Long and Happy Life. Thorndike Press Large Print, 2017.
17 Sinek, Simon, David Mead, and Peter Docker. Find Your Why: A Practical Guide for Discovering Purpose for You and Your Team. Penguin Books, 2017.
18 Brown, Brené. Rising Strong: The Reckoning. The Rumble. The Revolution. Random House, 2015.
19 Vilane, Sizwe. To The Top from Nowhere. Central Books Ltd, 2018.
20 Newman, Martyn. Emotional Capitalists: The Ultimate Guide to Developing Emotional Intelligence for Leaders. RocheMartin Institute, 2014.
21 Collins, Jim. Good to Great. Random House Business Books, 2001.
22 Leaf, Caroline. Switch On Your Brain: The Key to Peak Happiness, Thinking, and Health. Baker Books, 2010.
23 Clifton, Jim, and Jim Harter. It's the Manager. Gallup, 2019.
24 State of the Global Workplace: 2023 Report. Gallup, 2023. https://www.gallup.com/workplace/468829/state-global-workplace.aspx.
25 Kotter, John P., and James L. Heskett. Corporate Culture and Performance. The Free Press, 1992.
26 Newman, Martyn. Emotional Capitalists: The Ultimate Guide to Developing Emotional Intelligence for Leaders. RocheMartin Institute, 2014.
27 Tiryaki, Timothy. Leading With Culture: Building People-Centric High-Performing Organizations. Paperback ed. TellWell, January 2, 2024.
28 Van Edwards, Vanessa. You Are Contagious. TEDxLondon, 2018. https://www.ted.com/talks/vanessa_van_edwards_you_are_contagious.

29 Edmondson, Amy C. The Fearless Organization: Creating Psychological Safety in the Workplace for Learning, Innovation, and Growth. John Wiley & Sons, 2018.

30 Edmondson, Amy C. The Fearless Organization: Creating Psychological Safety in the Workplace for Learning, Innovation, and Growth. John Wiley & Sons, 2018.

31 Lencioni, Patrick M. The Five Dysfunctions of a Team: A Leadership Fable. Jossey-Bass, 2002.

32 Zak, Paul J. "The Neuroscience of High-trust Organizations." Harvard Business Review. 2018.

33 Zak, Paul J. "Trustworthiness: How Our Brains Decide When to Trust, Insights from Neuroscience." Harvard Business Review. 2019.

34 Zak, Paul J. "Trustworthiness: How Our Brains Decide When to Trust, Insights from Neuroscience." Harvard Business Review. 2019.

35 Tedeschi, Richard G., and Lawrence G. Calhoun. "The Posttraumatic Growth Inventory: Measuring the Positive Legacy of Trauma." Journal of Traumatic Stress 9, no. 3 (1996): 455-471.

36 Sheryl Sandberg and Adam Grant, Option B: Facing Adversity, Building Resilience, and Finding Joy (New York: Penguin Random House, 2017).

37 Future Forum Pulse. "Amid Spiking Burnout, Workplace Flexibility Fuels Company Culture and Productivity." Future Forum (Winter 2022/2023).

38 Klotz, Alexander, and Michelle C. Bolino. "When Quiet Quitting Is Worse Than the Real Thing." Harvard Business Review, 2022.

39 World Health Organization. "Burn-Out an 'Occupational Phenomenon': International Classification of Diseases." WHO, 2019.

40 Clifton, Jim, and Jim Harter. It's the Manager. Gallup, 2019.

41 Howatt, Greg, et al. "The Mental Health Commission of Canada Found That in Any Given Week, 500,000 Canadians Miss Work Due to a Psychological Health Issue." The Canada Life Assurance Company, 2022.

42 Future Forum Pulse. "Amid Spiking Burnout, Workplace Flexibility Fuels Company Culture and Productivity." Future Forum (Winter 2022/2023).

43 Donald Clifton and Jim Harter, Gallup Wellbeing at Work: How to Build an Engaged and Thriving Workforce (Gallup Press, 2020).

44 Csikszentmihalyi, Mihaly. Flow: The Psychology of Optimal Experience. Harper Perennial, 2008.
45 Dalton-Smith, Saundra. The 7 Types of Rest Every Person Needs. TED, 2021. https://www.ted.com/talks/saundra_dalton_smith_the_7_types_of_rest_every_person_needs.
46 Van der Kolk, Bessel A. The Body Keeps the Score: Brain, Mind, and Body in the Healing of Trauma. Penguin Books, 2014.
47 Maté, Gabor. When the Body Says No: Understanding the Stress-Disease Connection. Big Happy Family, 2011.
48 Nagoski, Emily, and Amelia Nagoski. Burnout: The Secret to Unlocking the Stress Cycle. Ballantine Books, 2019.
49 Leaf, Caroline. Switch On Your Brain: The Key to Peak Happiness, Thinking, and Health. Baker Books, 2010.
50 Lee, Michelle. A Journey to Life. Self-published, 2023.

Manufactured by Amazon.ca
Acheson, AB